MACMILLAN MASTER GUIDES

GENERAL EDITOR: JAMES GIBSON

JANE AUSTEN	*Emma* Norman Page
	Sense and Sensibility Judy Simons
	Persuasion Judy Simons
	Pride and Prejudice Raymond Wilson
	Mansfield Park Richard Wirdnam
SAMUEL BECKETT	*Waiting for Godot* Jennifer Birkett
WILLIAM BLAKE	*Songs of Innocence and Songs of Experience* Alan Tomlinson
ROBERT BOLT	*A Man for All Seasons* Leonard Smith
CHARLOTTE BRONTË	*Jane Eyre* Robert Miles
EMILY BRONTË	*Wuthering Heights* Hilda D. Spear
GEOFFREY CHAUCER	*The Miller's Tale* Michael Alexander
	The Pardoner's Tale Geoffrey Lester
	The Wife of Bath's Tale Nicholas Marsh
	The Knight's Tale Anne Samson
	The Prologue to the Canterbury Tales Nigel Thomas and Richard Swan
JOSEPH CONRAD	*The Secret Agent* Andrew Mayne
CHARLES DICKENS	*Bleak House* Dennis Butts
	Great Expectations Dennis Butts
GEORGE ELIOT	*Middlemarch* Graham Handley
	Silas Marner Graham Handley
	The Mill on the Floss Helen Wheeler
T. S. ELIOT	*Selected Poems* Andrew Swarbrick
HENRY FIELDING	*Joseph Andrews* Trevor Johnson
E. M. FORSTER	*Howards End* Ian Milligan
WILLIAM GOLDING	*The Spire* Rosemary Sumner
	Lord of the Flies Raymond Wilson
OLIVER GOLDSMITH	*She Stoops to Conquer* Paul Ranger
THOMAS HARDY	*The Mayor of Casterbridge* Ray Evans
	Tess of the d'Urbervilles James Gibson
BEN JONSON	*Volpone* Michael Stout
JOHN KEATS	*Selected Poems* John Garrett
PHILIP LARKIN	*The Whitsun Weddings* and *The Less Deceived* Andrew Swarbrick
D.H. LAWRENCE	*Sons and Lovers* R. P. Draper
HARPER LEE	*To Kill a Mockingbird* Jean Armstrong
GERARD MANLEY HOPKINS	*Selected Poems* R. J. C. Watt
CHRISTOPHER MARLOWE	*Doctor Faustus* David A. Male
THE METAPHYSICAL POETS	Joan van Emden

MACMILLAN MASTER GUIDES
LORD OF THE FLIES
BY WILLIAM GOLDING

RAYMOND WILSON

First published 1986 by
MACMILLAN PRESS LTD
Houndmills, Basingstoke, Hampshire RG21 6XS
and London
Companies and representatives
throughout the world

ISBN 0–333–40409–2

A catalogue record for this book is available
from the British Library.

Printed and bound in Great Britain by
Antony Rowe Ltd, Chippenham and Eastbourne

CONTENTS

GENERAL EDITOR'S PREFACE

The aim of the Macmillan Master Guides is to help you to appreciate the book you are studying by providing information about it and by suggesting ways of reading and thinking about it which will lead to a fuller understanding. The section on the writer's life and background has been designed to illustrate those aspects of the writer's life which have influenced the work, and to place it in its personal and literary context. The summaries and critical commentary are of special importance in that each brief summary of the action is followed by an examination of the significant critical points. The space which might have been given to repetitive explanatory notes has been devoted to a detailed analysis of the kind of passage which might confront you in an examination. Literary criticism is concerned with both the broader aspects of the work being studied and with its detail. The ideas which meet us in reading a great work of literature, and their relevance to us today, are an essential part of our study, and our Guides look at the thought of their subject in some detail. But just as essential is the craft with which the writer has constructed his work of art, and this may be considered under several technical headings - characterisation, language, style and stagecraft, for example.

The authors of these Guides are all teachers and writers of wide experience, and they have chosen to write about books they admire and know well in the belief that they can communicate their admiration to you. But you yourself must read and know intimately the book you are studying. No one can do that for you. You should see this book as a lamppost. Use it to shed light, not to lean against. If you know your text and know what it is saying about life, and how it says it, then you will enjoy it, and there is no better way of passing an examination in literature.

JAMES GIBSON

ACKNOWLEDGEMENTS

The author and publishers wish to thank the following who have kindly given permission for the use of copyright material:

Faber & Faber Limited and the Putnam Publishing Group Inc. for extracts from *Lord of the Flies* by William Golding.

Cover illustration: *The Plains of Heaven*, by John Martin. ©Tate Gallery Publications.

1 WILLIAM GOLDING:
LIFE AND BACKGROUND

William Golding was born in Cornwall in 1911, and was, therefore, a child during the Great War of 1914-18, which cast a dark shadow on the prevailing optimism, derived from the Victorian period, about human progress. He attended Marlborough Grammar School, and from there went up to Oxford, originally with the intention of reading science, though he switched subjects and graduated in English in 1933. Like his father before him, he became a teacher. In 1939 he married, and a year later volunteered for the Royal Navy, in which he served until 1945. He saw action, took part in the D-Day landings in Normandy, and rose to the rank of lieutenant. After the war he returned to teaching, taking a post at Bishop Wordsworth's School, Salisbury, a boys' school. In 1954, *Lord of the Flies*, his first published novel, met with some critical attention, but it was not until 1962 that he was able to retire from teaching to become a full-time author. His publications are: *Lord of the Flies*, 1954 (made into a film in 1963); *The Inheritors*, 1955; *Pincher Martin*, 1956; a play, *The Brass Butterfly*, 1958; *Free Fall*, 1959; *The Spire*, 1964; *The Hot Gates*, 1965; *The Pyramid*, 1967; *The Scorpion God*, 1971; *Darkness Visible*, 1979; *Rites of Passage*, 1980; *A Moving Target*, 1982; *The Paper Men*, 1984. Several universities have conferred Honorary Doctorate Degrees on him. He won the James Tait Black Memorial Prize and the Booker McConnell in 1980, and in 1984 he was given the Nobel Prize for Literature, the highest of all literary awards.

It is worth noting some major influences on Golding. As a child, he read such books as *The Pilgrim's Progress*, *Gulliver's Travels*, *Robinson Crusoe*, *The Coral Island* and *Tarzan of the Apes* with delight and admiration. Their influence – or his reaction against their influence – extends into his mature writing. But the action he saw during his time in the Navy made a lasting impression on him, too. 'The war was unlike any other fought in Europe,' he has said. 'It taught us not fighting, politics or the follies of nationalism, but about the given nature of man.' *Lord of the Flies*, like all his novels, is preoccupied with 'the given nature of man'. It testifies to the violence of war that he has experienced in himself, as well as witnessing it in others. At the same time, *Lord of the Flies* bears witness to the influence of his years of schoolteaching, during which he not only acquired an accurate ear for how boys speak, but a profound understanding of how they think and feel – an understanding that is at the heart of the novel.

2 R. M. BALLANTYNE'S
THE CORAL ISLAND (1858)

In *Lord of the Flies* William Golding twice refers to *The Coral Island*. In chapter 2, Ralph voices the initial enthusiasm of all the boys stranded on an island free of adults, when he declares that it is all 'like a book'. At once there is a clamour all around him:

> '*Treasure Island* —— '
> '*Swallows and Amazons* —— '
> '*Coral Island* —— '

The titles are well known to every schoolboy, and what they imply is, as Ralph says, that until the grown-ups come to fetch them, they'll 'have fun'. The second reference to Ballantyne's story is at the very end of the novel, when the naval officer comes to the rescue, and Ralph stammers out that the boys, who now appear like young savages, had at first tried to live decent civilised lives. 'I know,' the officer replies. 'Jolly good show. Like the Coral Island.'

It is no accident that *The Coral Island* should be explicitly referred to near the beginning and at the end of *Lord of the Flies*, since William Golding by intention set himself to write an island story that deliberately challenges Ballantyne's. This is obvious from what he says in an unpublished letter:

> I said to Ann [Golding's wife] in about 1953, 'Wouldn't it be a good idea to write a book about real boys on an island, showing what a mess they'd make?' She said, 'That *is* a good idea!' So I sat down and wrote it.

Apart from *Treasure Island* and *Swallows and Amazons*, there are literally dozens of other novels within the adventure-island-story tradition, among which Defoe's *Robinson Crusoe* and Wyss's *Swiss Family Robinson* are most extensively read still; but of all these stories it is *The Coral Island* that Golding takes as his model for all that he attacks as unrealistic in the tradition. What he gives us, then, is a story that inverts the facile assumptions and values of Ballantyne's optimistic fiction, and Golding even goes so far in parody as to use the identical names Ballantyne uses for his own main characters. Jack and Ralph are protagonists in both *The Coral Island* and *Lord of the Flies*, while Peterkin, the third boy in Ballantyne, emerges as two boys, Peter and Simon, in Golding's story. Fully to appreciate *Lord of the Flies* we need to read *The Coral Island*, or at least to understand its theme and treatment.

The Coral Island begins with a wreck, as does *Lord of the Flies*, and with survivors cast onto a tropical island. The island has everything necessary to sustain human life and the survivors can therefore show their resourcefulness by creating a small community from scratch, free from the constraints of the adult world.

Everything about Ballantyne's boys, who are older by some years than Golding's boys, is confident and positive. They are clean, upstanding *British* boys, who work co-operatively and loyally to uphold the best colonial traditions. They never for a moment forget that they are representatives of a nation with the greatest empire on earth and they virtually make their island into an imperial outpost. In Eden-like surroundings they pool the contents of their pockets for tools to tackle the jobs that lie ahead: they ingeniously exploit every natural resource, erect a 'rustic bower', 'luxuriate on the fat of the land', build and provision a small boat which they triumphantly navigate in exploring nearby islands, and generally do full credit to themselves by creating a society at least as fully civilised as that of middle-class Victorian England.

The reason Ralph gives for their success is the moral centre of the novel:

> . . . we three on this our island, although most unlike in many things, when united, make a trio so harmonious that I question if there ever met before such an agreeable triumvirate. There was, indeed, no note of discord whatever in the symphony we played together on that sweet Coral Island; and now I am persuaded that this was owing to our having been all tuned to the same key, namely, that of *love*! Yes, we loved one another with much fervency while we lived on that island; and, for that matter, we love each other still. (*The Coral Island*, ch. 14)

There is nothing wrong with the sheer *decency* of the shipwrecked boys, but because this decency is unqualified and unrelated to other dimensions of character, they fail to convince and are merely emblematic. In unselfconsciously addressing one another as 'my dear boy' or 'my dear fellow' they set the tone for a novel which has, among its characteristic vocabulary, the substantives 'joy', 'wonder' and 'delight', and the adjectives 'jolly', 'cheery' and 'hearty', while much time is spent throughout in exclamatory 'hurrahs!' over the scenery and a variety of fauna and flora.

Since it so perfectly mirrors the assumptions and values of its period, Victorians may well have considered *The Coral Island* realistic, not least in its portrayal of the boys. In affirming progress, imperialism, self-reliance, the Creator, the goodness of nature and of human nature (when Christianised, at least), the book must have struck contemporary readers, who took these things for granted, as true to life. But for us, the novel is a gallimaufry of high adventure, natural history and didactic moralising, with some occasional clowning for light relief.

The moral world of *The Coral Island* is utterly naïve. Ballantyne is prepared to recognise evil, but he identifies it exclusively with savagery and black skin. This island which makes the boys wonder 'whether Adam and Eve had found Eden more sweet' is visited by warring cannibals who very creditably live up to their reputation by slaughtering one another wholesale, by tearing a child from its mother's arms and hurling it into the sea, and by banqueting on 'long pig' (the human body). Evil abruptly invades Paradise. But significantly it comes from *outside*. The boys are no more than witnesses and spectators of it, though the shrewd reader will note that Ralph cannot look away:

> ... I felt my heart grow sick at the sight of this bloody battle, and would fain have turned away, but a species of fascination seemed to hold me down and glue my eyes upon the combatants.

This fascination with evil hints that something *inside* Ralph is responsive to it; but that is as far as Ballantyne can go in acknowledging that dark forces may lurk in his boy heroes.

Finally, while acting as 'true knights' to save a native woman of 'gentle expression' (her skin predictably is lighter than the rest), Jack, Ralph and Peter are themselves captured by savages, who plan to eat them. These black savages provide the novel's vocabulary of evil; they are variously called 'demons', 'monsters' and 'incarnate fiends', and it is said of them that 'Beelzebub himself could hardly desire better company'. (Translated, the word 'Beelzebub' means 'lord of the flies'.) The fate of Ballantyne's boys appears sealed, unless, as Ralph says, 'the Almighty puts forth His arm' to save them; and this, of course, He does. Miraculously, a missionary turns up and in no time at all converts the savages, who immediately renounce what Ballantyne calls their 'natural depravity'. They become instant Christians, honest traders and shake hands like true Britons with Jack, Ralph and Peter, who 'have nothing more to do but get ready for sea... and hurrah for dear old England!'

Without some grasp of Ballantyne's story we cannot really appreciate how extensively Golding parodies and satirises and mocks his model. His boys have nothing in common with the idealised boys of *The Coral Island*, except their initial joy in finding themselves free of adults on a tropical island. Thereafter, they increasingly deviate from Ballantyne's model heroes. They fail to co-operate, lack practical sense, are afflicted with diarrhoea and tormented by nightmares and fear of a beast. Physically and morally, they degenerate, becoming filthy in their habits and their imaginings, until at last they turn into murderous savages.

In turning to a chapter-by-chapter analysis of the book, we can trace step by step this descent into savagery.

3 SUMMARIES AND
CRITICAL COMMENTARY

Chapter 1

Summary

The novel opens with a twelve-year-old boy, Ralph, picking his way through an area of devastated jungle. Presently he hears a voice calling to him and another boy scrambles out of the undergrowth to join him. This boy is similar in age to Ralph, but there all similarity ends. Ralph is fair and attractive, with a boxer's physique, in sharp contrast to his new companion, who is stumpy, bespectacled, very fat and asthmatic. From their talk we learn that they are evacuees from an atomic war, and have escaped from the passenger-tube dropped onto the jungle by an aircraft which was under attack and on fire. The scar in the jungle has been made by this tube, which after landing was dragged by a storm out to sea, where it sank, with some children still aboard; but some other children must, like themselves, have made their escape. Ralph naively supposes the pilot will return, but the fat boy knows better, and is alarmed by the realisation that no adults have survived. The same realisation excites and exhilarates Ralph.

Their talk, as they make their way to the beach, illustrates their differences still more. Ralph is middle-class in speech, background and manner. He is distantly reserved towards the fat boy, whose speech is ungrammatical and whose background is much inferior to his own. Reaching the palm-fringed shore, Ralph pulls off his school uniform and sprawls on the beach. The fat boy delays to eat fruit in the jungle, but follows Ralph and confidentially reveals the secret that his hated nickname at school was Piggy. This strikes Ralph as hilarious, and even after he finds an ideal pool in which to swim and dive, he continues to reject Piggy's attempts to make friends by taunting him with his nickname. Piggy cannot swim but sits up to his neck in the water, trying to be companionable.

They climb out of the lagoon, put on their clothes and clamber onto a shelf or platform of pink granite in the shade of young palm trees. Piggy thoughtfully points out that they may never be rescued, not even by Ralph's father, who, though a naval commander, is ignorant of their whereabouts. He urges action: 'We got to find the others. We got to do something.' Ralph remains dreamy and indifferent, but suddenly notices an object lying in the lagoon, and Piggy identifies it as a conch shell. When they fish it out of the water and weeds, Piggy babbles on about its use: properly blown into, it gives a booming note that can be used to summon other evacuees who may have survived. Ralph blows several blasts and first one, then a straggle of boys, more or less in their school uniforms still, emerge from the surrounding forest and from the heat haze of the beach. They crowd around Ralph expectantly. Then out of the heat haze comes a party of boys marching in step and wearing the black cloaks and caps of choirboys. Their leader is a red-haired boy called Jack Merridew. He is indifferent to one of his choristers, Simon, who faints, and hostile to Piggy, whom he calls Fatty. Ralph wins popularity by revealing Piggy's nickname, but then makes the serious suggestion that they ought to have a chief. Jack, who is almost as old as Ralph, stakes his own claim to be chief. Piggy apart, the other boys are all younger, the smallest of them being about five years old. Roger suggests a vote, but despite the choir, who support Jack's claim with 'dreary obedience', Ralph is voted for by the majority and accepts the leadership.

In a gesture of goodwill, Ralph tells Jack he can keep the choir, and Jack immediately announces they will be an army of hunters. Ralph decides that they should explore their surroundings to find out if they are on an island. He appoints Jack and Simon to accompany him, disappointing Piggy, whom he realises he has hurt. Under Ralph's orders Piggy stays behind to check the names of the survivors. The three boys are excited as they make their way through the jungle and climb the hill beyond, discovering animal tracks and laughing and shouting with the joy of explorers. Half way up to the summit they heave a great rock down into the jungle, then mount upward, to stand on the square top, from which they can see that they are in fact on an island, with a coral reef lying a mile beyond the beach on which they assembled. All three of them share a sense of triumph and uplift at having an island all of their own. Back they scramble to the beach, but pause twice on the way, to examine the exotic candle bushes, then to uncover a small pig entangled in creepers. Jack draws his knife, but fails to kill the pig, which escapes. They all know that the real reason for this failure is the horror they all feel about killing a living creature. Jack, however, swears that next time he will be merciless.

Commentary

The novel begins, as it will end, by emphasising what very small boys the characters are. Ralph, at twelve years and a few months, is the oldest and biggest of them, but there is something forlorn in his first appearance: he is dishevelled, with drooping stockings, as he picks his way through the forest to the lagoon, trailing behind him his school sweater. We recognise here that even Ralph is small and rather helpless, but as the story unfolds, we cease to be so conscious of how very young all the boys are. The author, in presenting their emotions, thoughts and actions, writes so skilfully that he penetrates to what is basic in human nature, not simply as it reveals itself in children, but as it reveals itself in adults, too.

Piggy next appears on the scene. Of all the boys, he is closest to the adult world, the standards of which he constantly strives to uphold; but even so, he is young enough to be wearing short trousers. Significantly, his first question is: 'Where's the man with the megaphone?' This refers back to someone on the plane who had charge of the evacuees, but the question arises partly because Piggy cannot see very well, despite his thick spectacles, and partly because he wants to be reassured that adults are among the survivors. When it seems that no adult has survived, the contrast between Piggy's alarmed reaction and Ralph's delight at realising a boyish ambition to shake off adult authority is as pronounced as all the other differences, physical and social, between the two boys.

The conversation between Ralph and Piggy fails to give us a very exact idea of what has happened. In view of Golding's precision in writing, and his meticulous concern for detail, this is surprising. Clearly, the boys were dropped into the jungle in a passenger-tube. The aircraft itself seems to have been shot down. But what exactly happened once the tube smashed into the jungle is curiously obscure. Piggy and Ralph, like the other boys who will soon join them, have apparently escaped from the tube before a raging storm dragged it out to sea, with some boys still aboard. One might have supposed that those boys who managed to escape would have clung together, but the majority are, in fact, quite widely dispersed. On the other hand, the choirboys remain an intact unit under Jack's command. We are left uncertain about the exact sequence of events and the time-scale. Of course, it can be argued that such details need not bother us: the author simply wants to plant the boys on an island and get on with his story, which is what really matters. This is true; but it is none the less odd that an author who is so punctilious about detail that he notes the 'multitude of raindrops' falling from the disturbed foliage after the storm, should be so vague about the major events that occurred while it raged.

The literary convention of isolating people on an island enables the author to examine how humans behave away from the influences of civilised society, and by choosing only children as characters Golding further uncomplicates his task, since they are not so completely steeped in sophisticated conventions as adults are. It would be a mistake, however, to imagine that Golding's children are wholly natural and innocent: on the contrary, they have been influenced for good and ill by the society in which they have grown up, even if they are less complex than adults. Just as Ralph jerks up his stockings and makes 'the jungle seem for a moment like the Home Counties', so, like his sophisticated elders, he plays at one-upmanship with Piggy, boasting about his father when Piggy has none, disdainfully withholding his name, and gradually stepping up his abuse of Piggy's 'ass-mar' and aunt. When we are introduced to the other boys, we are quickly aware of their cruel attitudes towards Piggy's infirmities, of Jack's arrogance and ambition, of the choirboys' sullenness towards Jack. But if they have many of the faults of their elders, they have some adult merits, too: both Ralph and Piggy show concern for the 'littluns'; there is a fleeting 'shy liking' between the rivals, Ralph and Jack; democracy is upheld in the vote they take and the conch shell is invested with the group's respect for law and order.

It is also worth noting that, though the island is in some respects a paradise, it is by no means perfect. Quite apart from its being 'scarred' by the passenger-tube – an injury that comes from the world of men – the island suffers the violence of natural storms; nor does nature spare the trapped piglet the prospect of a slow death from starvation. In later chapters we learn more about the squalid swarms of flies, and the decay and rottenness of the forest; but even in the first chapter, which most closely resembles the Eden-like world of R. M. Ballantyne's *The Coral Island*, Golding carefully avoids idealising either nature or human nature.

In fact, we are given indications of what lies ahead for the boys in some seemingly incidental references: for example, there is a hint of menace in the 'skull-like coco-nuts' lying under the palms, and in the way Jack slashes candle buds with his knife, and in the image of a 'black, bat-like creature' dancing under the advancing body of a boy. Still more sinister is the emergence from the mirage of a troop of choirboys who come to perch 'like black birds' near Ralph, 'their bodies, from throat to ankle...hidden by black cloaks...'. Golding is much too subtle a craftsman to obtrude on the reader what such images may portend, and we may not be fully conscious of their cumulative effect upon us; nevertheless, they insidiously influence our response to the text. Even a negative statement can contribute to the tone and atmosphere of the narrative, as when we are told there is 'a mildness about [Ralph's] mouth and eyes that proclaimed *no devil* (my italics). This has an implication that is made clearer in what is said about Jack:

His face was crumpled and freckled, and ugly without silliness. Out of this face stared two light blue eyes, frustrated now, and turning, or ready to turn, to anger.

The first chapter comes closest to capturing something of the heady atmosphere of Ballantyne's novel. Piggy apart, the boys feel that to be liberated from adults is exhilarating: Ralph stands on his head, has a mock fight with Simon, and the trio who explore the island express their joy in cries of fifties slang (Wacco, Wizard and Smashing), now rather dated. They are bright-eyed and held by 'a kind of glamour'; they rejoice that the island is all theirs; their senses are intoxicated and the triumph they feel unites them in happiness. Even so, their ascent of the hill (Golding calls it a mountain, inviting us to see it through the eyes of small boys) is interrupted by Jack's need to heave a great rock into the forest below – a piece of wanton violence. This, together with Jack's fury with himself when his nerve fails him in his attempt to kill the piglet, points ominously to what the future might hold.

Chapter 2

Summary
Ralph blows the conch and the boys gather to hear him report on what he, Jack and Simon have discovered by climbing to the top of the hill. They are, he tells them, alone on an uninhabited island. Jack quickly interrupts to insist that an army is still necessary – for hunting pigs; and when they describe how the piglet escaped, Jack again slams his knife into a tree trunk, muttering about 'next time'. Ralph agrees that hunters are needed, but tries to put over the serious message that since there are no grown-ups, they will have to behave responsibly and look after themselves. Shouting out will not do: hands must be raised by those wishing to say something, 'like at school', then the conch can be handed over to whichever boy is entitled to speak. Jack enthusiastically supports this. He wants rules, and punishment for anyone who breaks them.

Piggy takes the conch. He remonstrates with the boys because they will not face up to the most important fact about their position, and challenges them with the question: 'Who knows we're here?' Their answers are silly and he insists that nobody knows where they are. Ralph takes back the shell and drives home Piggy's message by repeating that they are all on their own and cut off from help, which could be a long time in coming. Knowledge of this stuns the assembly into silence as the evening begins to close in around them. Ralph tries to reassure them that they are on 'a good island', with food and drink, so that they can have 'a good time' while waiting to be rescued. He says their situation is 'like in a book', and they all respond excitedly, naming their favourite island adventure stories.

One of the smallest boys, only six years old and with a 'mulberry-coloured birthmark' on one side of his face, is encouraged by the boys around him to say what is worrying him. He is pushed towards Ralph and holds out his hands for the conch. Everyone laughs, and he starts to cry; but Ralph gives him the conch, and Piggy, kneeling to hear what the child is muttering through his tears, interprets for him. The child fears 'a snake-thing', a 'beastie' that wants to eat him and that he claims to have seen in the woods. The boys stir uneasily, but Ralph explains that there can be no beast on the island; that it could not have been seen anyway, if it came in the dark; and that the whole thing was only a bad dream. This reasoning apparently satisfies the older boys, but fails to convince the small ones. Meanwhile, the child with the birthmark says the snake-thing turns into a jungle creeper during the day, but re-emerges in the dark. Ralph tries in vain to reassure the assembly, and when Jack seizes the conch and declares that although there is no snake, he and his hunters will hunt it down, matters are made still worse. Exasperated, Ralph repeatedly denies there is a beast, but his words carry no conviction with the boys.

Changing the subject, Ralph points out that although they will all have fun, they must ensure they are rescued, too. This everyone agrees with and Ralph goes on to explain how the Queen has a map of their island, and how a ship is bound to come to their aid. There is applause from everyone and Ralph explains how by making a fire they can attract the attention of passing ships. Led by Jack, the boys swarm away up the hill, ignoring Ralph's appeal for order and Piggy's disgusted disapproval of their childishness. Ralph follows and joins the rest, who are now gathering fuel for a fire under Jack's orders. Ralph and Jack co-operate in hauling a log to the fire; Piggy, disabled by his asthma, is slow to climb to where the wood is piled, ready to be lit. But Ralph blushes with embarrassment when he realises that he has no means of lighting the fire; he even appeals for matches. Then Jack snatches the spectacles from Piggy, who loudly protests, and they use the lenses to focus the rays of the setting sun on a piece of rotten wood, which smoulders into flame to the cheers of the crowd.

Soon the fire burns furiously. Many of the boys avoid its heat by sheltering behind rocks. Ralph, meanwhile, announces that the fire is useless, since it is all flame and no smoke, and Piggy agrees, only to be scorned by Jack. Because he holds the conch, Piggy tries to make a statement, but Jack says the conch 'doesn't count on the top of the mountain', and tells him to 'shut up'. Ralph intervenes, takes the conch himself, insists that it *does* count, anywhere, and says there should be 'special people' to tend the fire. Taking the conch, Jack agrees, stressing how important rules are, and how they must all do the right thing because they are English. He volunteers to use some of his hunters to keep the fire going, and to keep a lookout. This wins him applause, but there is no sign of a ship as the sun drops to the horizon, and Ralph again declares that they will eventually be rescued.

Clutching the conch, Piggy reproaches the assembly for not listening to his good advice; then he notices that on the other, steeper side of the island, sparks have set the trees ablaze. The rapidly spreading fire swallows up acres of jungle. 'You got your small fire all right,' Piggy shouts at them, sarcastically, feeling powerless and frightened. The twins, watching smoke that stretches for miles, giggle at the thought of how they had all wanted smoke, and everyone shrieks with irresponsible laughter. Piggy alone remains solemn and tries to get them to see what their real responsibilities are: to build shelters, to keep a *proper* fire, to obey Ralph and to see that he, Piggy, is given a complete list of names.

Ralph is angry that Piggy has failed to obtain such a list, and Piggy defends himself, pointing out that the 'little'uns' behave uncontrollably. Some of them, he says, have wandered off to collect fruit where the fire is now raging. Where, he asks, is the child with the birth-mark? The silence is broken only by the roaring of the forest fire. The 'little'uns' scream 'Snakes! Snakes!' as they watch the creepers of a tree writhe in flame. They all know, without saying it, that the child has been burned alive, and the sun sinks below the sea's horizon.

Commentary
The chapter opens with another assembly. This is called on 'the platform' on which, significantly, *light* (associated with reason) is scattered. There are already indications of disarray among the boys and Ralph, holding the conch, seeks to establish order as they have known it by appealing to school discipline. Jack forgets for a moment his obsession with hunting pigs to call for rules, but in doing so he is, ironically enough, breaking the rule that forbids him to speak without the shell. Still more ironically and portentously, he takes satisfaction in threatening the rule-breakers with punishments. Only Piggy is aware that Jack's interruption is a distraction from what matters. He tries here, as so often he will try in the future, to focus Ralph's attention on what is vitally important – on the *realities* of their situation, which Ralph grasps only imperfectly; indeed, he cannot distinguish reality from books of adventure, the Queen's supposed maps and notions of inevitable rescue.

This lack of realism actually makes Ralph a popular leader, though there is some unease among the boys because of the snake or beastie reported by the boy with the birth-mark. Though the older boys deny there is any beastie at all, the little ones, as Golding notes, require 'more than rational assurance': an acknowledgement that there is something too deep in their natures to be reached by mere logic. And even the older boys are far from being rational. In the same breath in which he denies the snake's existence, Jack promises he will hunt it down and kill it! This angers Ralph, who time and again makes the point that there *is* no beast; but for all his vehemence the assembly is unconvinced and answers him with a brooding silence.

A clamour arises when Ralph announces the need for a fire and it is again Jack who breaks the rules, calling on others to follow him as he heads the mob in a disorderly scramble for wood. Piggy, whose illness and isolation have made him much more grown-up than the others, disgustedly blames them for 'acting like a crowd of kids', though a crowd of kids is exactly what they are! He even speaks of 'tea-time', as if the civilised order of English domestic life could continue on the island, only to find that Ralph has left him and joined the others in 'senseless ebullience'. The conch and the platform, both symbols of order, are abandoned.

When Ralph joins Jack in gathering logs for the fire, we are given a brief glimpse of their sharing a happy experience, as their namesakes constantly do in *The Coral Island*:

> Once more, amid the breeze, the shouting, the slanting sunlight on the high mountain, was shed that glamour, that strange invisible light of friendship, adventure, and content.

Both boys share this happiness in a common task; but the 'invisible light of friendship', like the sun's 'slanting light', will be quickly extinguished. It is only at the very beginning of their stay on the island that Ralph releases his exuberant spirits by turning cartwheels.

Confronted with the problem of how to set fire to the pile of gathered wood and leaves, Ralph and Jack share an acute embarrassment. They regard themselves as leaders and both blush at the 'shameful knowledge' of their incompetence. There is absurdity and pathos in Ralph's asking if anyone has matches. Finally it is Jack who solves the problem, seizing Piggy's spectacles without apology or permission, and using them as a burning glass (Golding slips up on a detail here: the lenses necessary to correct short-sightedness do not concentrate, but disperse, light). Piggy, in fact, is never once treated by Jack as an individual with rights: he is wholly beneath Jack's contempt. The spectacles are eventually thrust back into Piggy's hands by Ralph, who may not always be a good leader, though he at least tries to behave justly. Simon, never less than compassionate in his understanding of everyone, attempts to reconcile Jack to Piggy by pointing out how useful Piggy's spectacles have been to them all. But Jack's fierce intolerance of Piggy is only strengthened by Piggy's more mature awareness of where they have gone wrong with the fire; he commands Piggy to 'shut up', and denies that the shell counts 'on top of the mountain'. Though loud in shouting for rules, he is the first to break them; but we should note that Ralph has courage enough to side with Piggy, in flat contradiction of Jack: 'Where the conch is, that's a meeting.' Instead of resenting this, as we might expect, Jack takes the conch and speaks like one of Ballantyne's boys, denying that they are savages, insisting on rules, and boasting: 'We're English; and the English are best at everything.' When he volunteers to split up the choir into fire-keepers and hunters, the authority of the conch shell and the law and order it represents seem to be restored and their future guaranteed.

This is illusory. In a paragraph of vivid images, Golding describes the forest fire, which runs as wild as the boys themselves did when they stormed the hilltop. The drum-roll of the fire frightens them all into silence, and even Ralph is made 'savage' by it, snarling at the sarcastic Piggy to 'shut up'. The fire is 'splendid, awful' (in the sense of inspiring awe), and Piggy nervously sees it as 'hell' – a hell let loose by the folly of undisciplined schoolboys. Tension is released only when the twins giggle, though their giggling and the shrieking laughter it provokes are touched with hysteria.

Only Piggy stands aloof, reproaching everyone for not helping Ralph, and pleading for a rational ordering of their activities. They do not have even a list of names! This triggers off a disturbing question, which leaves Piggy gasping in an asthma attack brought on by terror. He asks where the little boy with the birth-mark is, and suddenly they all know he has been consumed in the hell-fire they themselves have made. The little ones (or 'littluns' as they come to be called) scream as a tree explodes in flame and the suggestion of their inhabiting hell, like young demons, is reinforced by their screaming and wailing, with faces 'lit redly from beneath'. As the drum-roll persists, we sense how portentous it is, threatening the boys' future.

By the time we reach this point in the book we cannot fail to notice how Golding's description of apparently *external* things and events runs parallel to the boys' internal dispositions, moods and fears. This is apparent from the way Golding gives us constant reminders about the drawing in of the day and the encroaching night. The symbolism is obvious, since shadows and night are traditionally charged with suggestions of fear and evil. But we should note that the references to the closing in of the darkness are constantly associated with the darkening mood of the boys. Golding draws attention to the 'decline of the sun', and with it the 'wandering breezes' that give a 'little coolness'; then he continues: 'The boys felt it and stirred restlessly'. Here, the physical reaction of the boys is indistinguishable from the terror that grips them. If they shudder, it is as much because of 'the snake-thing' as because of the breeze. It is by no means an accident that Roger declares they may never be rescued just as the sun slides 'nearer and nearer the sill of the world'. Similarly, as their hopes of rescue fade and they realise that the first of their number is dead, the sun ominously slips below the horizon, giving way to night.

Chapter 3

Summary
Jack, determined to succeed as a hunter, minutely examines the forest floor for signs of pigs. Except for his tattered shorts, he is naked. All his senses are tensed and his fanaticism shows in his eyes, which are 'nearly mad'. He finds a pig-run, hears the movement of pigs and hurls his spear in their direction, only to be mocked by the sound of the pigs making off. Cursing, he returns to the beach, where Ralph, aided by Simon, is trying not very successfully to erect a shelter.

Ralph cannot believe so little has been accomplished. After days of trying to set up shelters, two are at best only precariously upright, while the one he is working on is 'in ruins'. He complains to Jack that he gets no co-operation: the littluns self-indulgently swim, eat and play, and the older ones are scarcely better. Jack claims exemption for his hunters and Simon suggests Ralph should call another meeting to lay the law down; but meetings, Ralph knows, solve nothing. The boys enjoy the talk, but afterwards neglect their duties, to play or hunt.

In an argument between Ralph and Jack, it becomes clear that Ralph resents Jack and his hunters, who so far have neither helped with what Ralph sees is the real work, nor had the least success in hunting. Jack makes no concession; he is consumed by a passion to track down and kill a pig, and Ralph's reproach only maddens him. Anger flares between the two, and does not subside until Ralph changes the subject to the nightmares and fears of the littluns. As Simon hints, it is as if the island is not 'a good island', after all. The words recall the time when they explored the island as a trio, and for a moment they remember the joy they shared then. Relaxed now, Jack reveals a secret: that he, too, senses a frightening presence in the forest.

When Ralph talks of being rescued as the solution to their problems, it is plain that Jack has stopped thinking about it altogether. Killing a pig has higher priority with him. Ralph's priority is to be rescued, and therefore he insists that the fire must be carefully tended by the hunters;

but Jack is not even listening. All his thoughts are concentrated on how to kill pigs. Their anger with one another flares up again, till at last Jack reluctantly volunteers to help Ralph before bathing. Meanwhile Simon, whom they both consider an oddity, has disappeared, so together they turn their backs on work and make their way to the pool for a swim, each conscious of the huge differences separating them, and torn between love and hate for one another.

Simon has meanwhile walked purposefully towards the trees, followed by some littluns, for whom he reaches down fruit before making his solitary way into the dark depths of the jungle. There, behind a dense wall of creepers, he squeezes into a hiding place he has made his own. Looking out from it, he can see a forest clearing, and he remains perfectly still there, listening to the sounds of birds and insects, absorbed in the contemplation of the luxuriant shrubs and flowers and trees, and smelling their scents as the night closes in.

Commentary
Some time has passed: probably some weeks, and certainly long enough for Jack's hair to be 'considerably longer'. In the previous chapter, animal imagery was used to describe the rapidly spreading fire, but with a suggestion that the fire's animality paralleled the wild behaviour of the boys. This chapter goes further. Jack is presented as almost naked, shaggy-haired, and bent double, 'his nose only a few inches from the humid earth', where he drops on all fours 'dog-like', seeking traces of the pigs, and sniffing 'with flared nostrils'. These images obviously imply a regression on Jack's part, and when Golding refers to 'the abyss of ages' and sees him as 'a furtive thing, ape-like among the tangle of trees', this regression is given an evolutionary dimension: Jack seems to merge with primordial man.

We should note Golding's vivid description of detail. Even the pig droppings are described with a delicate precision, but this is exactly right, since Jack's obsession leads him to scrutinise them with a kind of loving care. As we read on, choices of word and image oblige us to see the action increasingly from Jack's viewpoint: for example, we are told in the first paragraph that he carries a 'sharpened stick', but in the third paragraph what he raises and hurls is a 'spear'.

Failing to kill a pig, Jack returns to the beach cursing, sweating, 'streaked with brown earth' and 'stained'. Later, he will *deliberately* paint himself. His frustration, meanwhile, does not help his temper, but Ralph is equally frustrated by his own inadequate efforts to erect shelters (unlike Ballantyne's boys, who effortlessly build a splendid bower), and a head-on row is inevitable. The littluns and hunters, infuriatingly for Ralph, are having fun, as he promised them they would;

but they do so at his expense and Simon's. Caught up in their separate frustrations, much of the talk between Ralph and Jack is *parallel* talk: what each one says fails even to register with the other. Ralph's tone is self-pitying and aggrieved; Jack's, more disturbingly, is one of rage and compulsion, since he is maddened and swallowed up by his need to kill. Only when they put aside their anger to talk of the littluns' fears, do Ralph and Jack begin to communicate, though they do so mostly in what is left unsaid and in broken sentences. Simon disregards their shameful feelings and speaks the words 'beastie' and 'snake', which are apparently taboo, just as any reference to the dead boy with the birthmark is taboo. They recall how good the island seemed when they first explored it, capturing for a moment 'the glamour of the first day', and laugh away any suggestion that it is otherwise. Ralph sees only a practical problem: to build shelters as a protection against storms and bad dreams alike. Jack shamefacedly confesses that when he is hunting in the forest he senses that he himself is being hunted down, 'as if something's behind' him. Trying to be grown-up, he pretends to dismiss this, though he is beset with doubt. As readers, we remember what has just been said about Jack's having a 'compulsion to track down and kill that was swallowing him up'. It is as if the compulsion to hunt that is destroying him is externalised in the 'something' tracking him from behind.

Staying practical, Ralph sees rescue as the only way out, but Jack has almost forgotten the word, and does not take seriously the responsibility for the fire. While Ralph talks earnestly about fire and rescue, Jack's face is 'rapt' in devising new plans to hunt and kill. Angry at Jack's monomania, Ralph reverts to his earlier complaints. Apart from Simon, no one helps him; and building shelters is work, not fun, like hunting. Jack grudgingly offers to lend a hand, but when they find Simon is missing, they abandon any idea of work and join the others swimming in the pool. As they walk towards it, Golding describes their alien identities in a telling metaphor: they are 'two continents of experience and feeling, unable to communicate'.

Simon has typically helped the littluns to fruit, before escaping, not into the communal fun of play and swimming, but into a secret place of his own, away from everyone. Here he can be at the still heart of the island's life, watching its colours, its fading 'honey-coloured sunlight' and stars coming out; hearing its every sound, including the coursing of his own blood through his body; smelling its decay and buds and flowers and 'scented air'. He has been the first to dare to suggest that the island may not be good, and he knows its secrets more intimately than any of the others; he is younger than Ralph and Jack; but he is unafraid.

Chapter 4

Summary
The boys adapt themselves to the life of the island. Their mornings are spent happily in play, but by noon the sun's heat is intolerable, creating strange mirages, which they learn to ignore; then comes a welcome coolness, accompanied by night, from the threat of which they huddle in the rickety shelters. Not everyone adapts equally well: Percival, a littlun, has stayed two days in the shelter and got a reputation for being 'batty' by his odd behaviour and constant crying. In general, the littluns are absorbed in their own separate but corporate living, though they suffer from eating unripe fruit, and still more from their fears of the dark.

Three littluns build and decorate sand-castles: Henry, the biggest of them, and Johnny and Percival, the two smallest boys. Johnny is well built and has 'a natural belligerence'; Percival is unattractive and badly adjusted. Two hunters come from tending the fire and cut across the beach to the pool. Roger comes first, deliberately trampling the sand-castles, followed by Maurice, who does the same. Percival whimpers, his eye full of sand, and Maurice hurries off, with a sense of guilt. Tears wash the sand from Percival's eye and he resumes play only to have Johnny throw more sand at him, so that he cries again. Henry tires of play and moves along the beach, shadowed by the forbidding figure of Roger. In the waters of the lagoon are minute creatures which drift with the tide, scavenging in the 'detritus of landward life'. Henry watches them and pokes about with a stick, absorbed and fulfilled in controlling the 'tiny transparencies'. Roger draws nearer. The evening breeze shakes down a cluster of large nuts about him, and by some association of ideas, he picks up stones and throws them all around Henry, but without aiming to hit him. Henry watches to find out where the stones come from, but Roger is too quick in hiding behind a tree. Laughing at being teased, Henry wanders off, leaving Roger curiously excited by his taunting.

Presently, Jack comes to get Roger, who blushes at being so nearly caught out. The pigs escape from them, Jack reasons, because they are easily seen, and he proceeds to camouflage himself with clay and charcoal in front of Roger and the twins, Sam and Eric, often called 'Samneric'. He dislikes his first attempt, but perseveres and finally, looking into a shell of water, is awed by the strange difference made by the camouflage. Hidden beind this mask, he is 'liberated from shame and self-consciousness', and dances around the others, laughing and snarling. They are awed and obedient as he leads them to the hunt.

At about this time Piggy discusses with Ralph the possibility of making a sundial, but he cannot fully explain how this can be done, and Ralph amuses himself by pulling Piggy's leg. Even among the biguns Piggy is regarded as an outsider. Ralph joins Maurice and Simon at the pool and after a while sees smoke on the horizon. He leaps up shouting, and the others share his excitement. But his hopes that their fire will attract the attention of the ship are dashed: there is no sign of a fire on the mountain. Ralph heads a mad scramble up the hill, only to pause half way up, agonising as to whether to go on, since if the fire is out, they will need Piggy's spectacles to rekindle it; but the slow-moving Piggy is far in the rear. Deciding to go on, he reaches the top, where the fire is dead. As the distant smoke fades away on the horizon, Ralph screams at the ship to come back.

Piggy is the last to struggle to the hill-top, from which, looking down onto the other, unfriendly side of the island, they see Jack at the head of the hunters, who climb towards them, chanting. Behind Jack the twins carry the carcass of a pig on a stake, and when the hunters reach Ralph, Piggy, Maurice and Simon, they shout out wildly about how they have killed the pig. Ralph ignores their boasting and complains that they have let the fire out – an unimportant and easily corrected matter, as far as Jack and his hunters are concerned. But Ralph withholds the appreciation Jack expects, sombrely repeating his accusation that the fire is out. Once more, the hunters shout aloud about the kill, the triumph and the blood, till Ralph points at the horizon and savagely declares there was a ship. He steps towards Jack, who faces him with a drawn knife. Piggy backs up Ralph, who pushes him aside, asserting that he is chief, and what he says goes. One of the small hunters wails and Jack hacks the pig with his knife to hide his embarrassment, while insisting they need meat. Ralph and Jack, 'the bloodied knife in his hand', angrily confront one another. Piggy again accuses Jack, who lashes out at him, knocking off his spectacles. When retrieved by Simon, one lens is broken, and Piggy impotently threatens Jack, who causes a laugh by mimicking Piggy's whining. Even Ralph is amused. While he has their good humour, Jack apologises for removing his hunters and letting the fire die.

The hunters see Jack's apology as 'handsome behaviour', but Ralph cannot just accept it conventionally: he still feels anger. Though Jack resents this, he is active in ordering another fire to be built, in an endeavour to compensate for what he has done. But Jack has nothing to light the fire with. Ralph, who has kept aloof, now borrows Piggy's spectacles, kindles a flame with them, and gives them back.

Ralph, despite himself, cannot resist joining in the feast. Piggy is refused meat by Jack, but surreptitiously given it by Simon. Jack, furious, then hurls a hunk of pig at Simon's feet. He shouts at the entire group, telling them that he has provided for everybody, and trying to win their sympathy for all that this has involved; but they show no more than a cool respect for him and their silence is broken only when Maurice asks about the killing. In their excitement at recounting the story, the boys re-enact what happened. Maurice pretends to be the pig; the rest crowd round him, threatening and chanting. Only when they tire does Ralph announce that he is going to call an assembly.

Commentary
The comparative coolness of the morning provides reassurance and a sense of reality to the boys, who can find pleasure in play. It is when the sun's heat beats savagely down that reality itself seems to dissolve: the firm outlines of the world about them seem to shift and mysteriously disintegrate. With the unreflecting acceptance of the young, the boys ignore what they cannot understand. The mirages create illusions that they take for reality by day, just as by night they take their tormented dreams for reality. This inability to distinguish between the real and the illusory accounts for a great deal of the story's subsequent action, and constitutes one of the novel's themes. Once 'the northern European tradition of work, play, and food' is violated by tropical conditions, nothing seems impossible any more.

The littluns are least of all able to keep a grip on reality, caught up as they are in their own 'passionately emotional and corporate life'. It is as if they have a group identity, but little awareness of themselves as individuals. That this is not wholly the case is apparent from the way in which Henry and Johnny, instructed by the vicious behaviour of the biguns, who kick sand in Percival's eyes, persist in persecuting a littlun who, like Piggy, is physically unattractive and unable to defend himself. Percival is treated as another outsider. A further insight into the minds of the littluns is afforded by Henry, who is 'absorbed beyond mere happiness' as he feels himself 'exercising control over living things'. There is more than a hint here that the exercise of physical dominance over weaker creatures is an instinct so deep in human nature that it manifests itself in early childhood, and is so potent a force that nothing else can equal or rival it. Ironically, while Henry rejoices in 'the illusion of mastery' over other creatures, Roger pelts the water around the younger child with stones, taunting him with superior power. We are given a gloss on Charles Darwin's bleak vision of the strong surviving at the expense of the weak. Meanwhile, all of this is a low-key anticipation of the novel's future action, in which Jack is driven to violence by his lust for power. There are restraints on exercising power in this chapter – first, when Maurice feels 'the unease of wrong-doing' after kicking sand into Percival's eye, and next, when Roger's arm is 'conditioned' by his upbringing from aiming stones directly at Henry. But such 'conditioning' weakens as time passes; and ironically, the civilisation that imposed it has not been able to control itself, and is in ruins.

Jack is obsessionally preoccupied with hunting, and he significantly equates hunting with war. Through camouflage, he disguises himself not simply from the others, who are 'appalled' by his transformation, but from himself, too, so that he appears to himself as 'an awesome stranger'. He hides behind this new mask, which liberated him 'from shame and self-consciousness' into savagery, and his laughter turns into a 'blood-thirsty snarling' before which Bill falls silent from terror. The word 'snarling' strongly hints at a reversion to an animal condition.

In sharp contrast, we see Piggy by the pool, struggling to express how he and Ralph might make a sundial, and therefore advocating not reversion, but progress, through an attempt to recreate an instrument belonging to both the adult world and to civilisation's evolution. Ralph, meanwhile, only mocks Piggy, who is without a sense of humour (perhaps because he is so often the butt of it). There is pathos in the way Piggy mistakes Ralph's amused leg-pulling for friendliness. Even to Ralph, Piggy remains an outsider, to be rudely dismissed for so futilely talking about rescue. Like a further bad joke at his expense, when smoke is seen on the horizon and rescue seems possible, Piggy alone is prevented by poor sight from seeing it.

Ralph's ravenous watching of the disappearing ship, his agonised indecision as to whether, when climbing to the fire, he should go back for Piggy's spectacles, and finally his hysterical screaming for the ship to come back, all reveal how desperately he recognises their need to be rescued, and equally their inability to cope on their own. His fury at the hunters for letting the fire go out is only intensified by the sight of them approaching with their kill, chanting in triumph. Simon, whose intuition is unfailing, looks from Ralph to Jack and is afraid. The hunters cannot wait to declare their victory and call out as they climb to the hilltop. Jack's hands are bloody, though he is still sufficiently 'conditioned' to grimace distastefully; he twitches as he claims he cut the pig's throat, and ambivalently laughs and shudders. What he expects is Ralph's approval: what he meets with is Ralph's total condemnation. The theme of power is restated. Jack is at first 'charitable in his happiness', but this happiness comes from his having 'out-witted a living thing', from his having imposed his will upon it, from his having 'taken away its life like a long satisfying drink'. When Ralph scorns this, repeating his reproaches about the fire, Jack's charitable impulse dies in anger and he confronts Ralph with his knife drawn; but his hand remains 'conditioned', and his triumph is further degraded when, realising what has happened, 'one of the smaller hunters [begins] to wail'.

The image in Chapter 3 of 'two continents of experience and feeling, unable to communicate' is paralleled by this new confrontation:

> The two boys faced each other. There was the brilliant world of hunting, tactics, fierce exhilaration, skill; and there was the world of longing and baffled common-sense.

When Piggy, driven by despair, speaks out against him, Jack lashes out at him in fury, because he dare not turn on Ralph. How fragile the things of civilisation are is shown when Piggy's spectacles, retrieved by Simon, whose actions are repeatedly gentle and understanding, are found to be broken on one side. But Simon apart, there is no sympathy for Piggy. On the contrary, Jack recovers some of his confidence by mocking Piggy's whining, and even Ralph is partly won over. When, on top of this, Jack offers a formal apology about the fire, he recovers his hunters' admiration, while Ralph, unable to respond at a merely conventional level, loses much of the moral initiative he had won for himself.

The struggle, largely psychological, between Ralph and Jack continues. By his resentful silence and refusal to move from where he stands, Ralph asserts his chieftainship again, to the frustration and anger of Jack. Ralph relents only to borrow Piggy's spectacles to light the fire others have prepared, and in returning them he obscurely realises that at this point he is dissociating himself from Jack for ever, and establishing a true relationship with Piggy. But the next victory in the struggle goes to Jack, once the pig is roasted and shared out, while Ralph and Piggy dribble in greed. Jack's attempt to deny Piggy meat is frustrated by Simon's self-sacrificing kindness, and this leads Jack to reassert his claim to be the provider for them all – a short step from claiming leadership. He wants desperately to be understood: he wants them all to appreciate what courage, what perseverance, what ingenuity, and what skill went into the killing of the pig. These spectacular qualities he implies are found in him, not in Ralph. But his angry plea for understanding fails: the boys respect him, but cannot truly comprehend his obsession.

Finally, the hunters re-enact the kill, ritualising, and therefore to an extent controlling, an event that they performed half in fear and half in pride. As they dance and chant, they resemble more and more a tribe of savages, and prefigure, in the mock killing of Maurice, the killing of Simon in Chapter 9.

Chapter 5

Summary
Ralph walks the beach, sorting out his confused thoughts, acknowledging his disillusion, and disgusted by his own dirty condition. As the

sun sets, he calls an assembly, to reassert his leadership and make the boys face the grim facts about their situation. Sitting on his tree trunk, with the others forming two sides of a triangle facing him, he tries hard to think straight before taking the conch and speaking. Piggy, as a protest at how he has been treated, stays for a time outside the triangle of boys, who are subdued because they feel guilt at having let the fire die.

Ralph explains that the assembly is called to 'put things straight'. This means *doing* things, not just talking about doing things. Specifically, he wants the rules observed concerning drinking water, lavatory arrangements and personal hygiene, and he reproaches them for their failure to help build the shelters and tend to the fire. Above all, he insists, the fire matters most, since without it they will not be rescued and will die. Speaking authoritatively, he demands their absolute obedience in this. Jack tries to interrupt him, protesting he talks too much, but Ralph will not yield. 'Things are breaking up,' Ralph warns, because of the fear they feel, particularly the littluns, but such fear is all nonsense.

Jack claims the conch and while overtly urging the littluns to put up with their fears, actually terrifies them with talk of a beast he says does not exist. Piggy speaks next, agreeing that there is no beast, but denying that there is any reason for fear, because life is 'scientific' and fear is imaginary, like ghosts: it does not exist unless people get frightened by other people. He challenges Phil, a littlun, to tell his story, in order to demonstrate how silly it is. Phil tells of a nightmare, and of waking in fear and seeing 'something big and horrid' in the forest. In an attempt to calm everyone, Ralph reasons that Phil was dreaming still, because nobody would go into the forest at night. But Simon confesses he has done so, which gives Jack a chance to ridicule him. The littluns laugh in a scared way, and Ralph orders Simon never to wander in the dark again.

The littluns push Percival forward and Ralph involuntarily recalls the boy with a birth-mark. But all Percival can do is repeat his name and address, then wail in misery. Other littluns start crying and Maurice distracts them by his mad clowning till they begin laughing. Jack, ignoring the rule about taking the conch, again talks about a beast, trying to force Percival to say where it is. Percival says it comes from the sea and falls into exhausted sleep. An eerie sensation is felt by all of them as they look at the dark waters of the lagoon and the sea beyond. They recall things said about sea monsters, and Ralph despairs, realising that his attempt to impose common sense and order has failed.

Simon tries ineffectually to tell the assembly that there may be a beast, though it is really inside themselves. He is howled down and struggles to find words to express his intuition of a flaw in human nature; but Jack makes a crude joke that humiliates Simon and sets everyone laughing. Piggy reaffirms his scientific faith, and Jack abuses him, too, and scuffles to possess the conch, which finally Ralph wrenches to himself. But it is too late. Ralph cannot suppress the talk about beasts and ghosts, and realises that he ought never to have held the assembly at dusk. He suggests voting, to decide whether ghosts exist or not, and when the vote goes against him, the common sense which he has clung to seems undermined. Piggy shouts out his protest, challenging them all to say whether they are human or savages or animals, while Jack abuses him and defies Ralph himself, by renouncing the rules of the assembly.

Finally, with talk about hunting the beast, Jack leaps from the platform and the boys, in disarray, follow him along the beach, where they begin their ritual dancing and chanting. Ralph is uncertain about everything, though Piggy speaks up for an adult world that makes sense, and both Simon and Piggy, aware that Jack is openly challenging Ralph, urge him to continue as chief. He tacitly agrees, but rejects Piggy's plea that he should blow the conch to reconvene the assembly, aware that he risks sacrificing the conch's authority forever, should it go unheeded. Then, as the three boys reassure one another about a responsible, adult world, and yearn for some 'sign' from it, they hear Percival wailing in his tormented sleep.

Commentary
Chapter 5 recapitulates several earlier events and themes. Most obviously, there are encroaching shadows and nightfall, as in Chapter 2, accompanied by a sense of terror, and Ralph recalls the forgotten boy burnt alive in the fire. But he recalls, too, his 'first enthusiastic exploration' of the island as 'part of a brighter childhood', and 'smiles jeeringly'. He is embittered by experience, for, instead of behaving honourably like the boys of *The Coral Island*, these boys have let themselves down in every imaginable way: they – and he – are dirty; and they are irresponsible, unco-operative, self-indulgent, and blinded by their short-term enjoyment of play and hunting to their own long-term good and the need to be rescued. Above all, the fears first voiced in Chapter 2 are examined again; but these have grown out of all rational proportion and are destroying the very possibility of sanity and order. Like Chapter 2, this chapter begins with an assembly, with what appears to be order and democratic procedure; and it ends, as Chapter 2 does, in a world of nightmare and disorder.

In calling an assembly, Ralph wishes both to re-establish his firm leadership, increasingly threatened by Jack, and to lay down the law about the rules by which they must live. His thoughts are 'a maze', and for the first time he acknowledges his respect for Piggy, who, though no leader, can think more clearly than he can himself. The 'tangle of

golden reflections' on the boys' faces leads him into unnerving specu-
lations about reality and unreality, but he recovers and addresses the
assembly with simple and direct logic, driving home his responsibilities
and their derelictions. But if he accuses the boys of being dirty, he does
so all the more earnestly because he recoils from the dirt clinging to
himself. Jack, on the other hand, is never self-critical. When Ralph
argues that fire and rescue are their only hope, Jack starts chipping
wood with his knife and whispering snidely to Robert. Next Jack
accuses Ralph of talking too much, and before the end of the chapter,
the boy who was loudest in demanding rules, with punishments for
their violation, disregards the conch, plays on the superstitious fears of
the littluns, assaults Piggy again, openly challenges Ralph's leadership,
and breaks up the assembly with cries of 'Bollocks to the rules!'

Though he has neither Piggy's gift as a thinker nor Simon's unerring
intuition, Ralph recognises, without being able to understand, that
things are falling apart; he even grasps that the break-up of sanity is
brought about by fear, the examination of which is the central concern
of this chapter. Jack sees fear as some sort of bad dream. It is a fact of
life that has to be put up with, and that is the end of the matter. Ralph
admits he sometimes feels fear, but declares it is mere nonsense, since
there is no objective cause for it. He shows little judgement when he
imagines that to bring the boys' fears into the open for public discussion will be a sufficient recipe for their cure, and still less when he ludicrously tries to discredit ghosts by a democratic vote. Piggy denies the
reality of fear. For him, it is ignorant superstition, incompatible with
science and the adult world which together constitute a true reality.
His attitude is essentially the priggish attitude expressed by one of
Ballantyne's boys:

> I neither believe in ghosts nor feel uneasy. I never saw a ghost
> myself and I never met anyone who had; and I have generally
> found that strange and unaccountable things have always been
> accounted for, and found to be quite simple, on close examina-
> tion.

As for the other boys, they are willing to locate fear in an animal, or
beast, or sea-monster, or ghost – anywhere, in fact, except in themselves!

It is Simon, and Simon alone, who gropes to a recognition that the
fear leading to the disintegration of their world is finally not external
to them, but ingrained in themselves. Piggy has no real understanding of
this when, speaking personally and with Jack in mind, he admits 'we get
frightened of people'. How far he is from sharing Simon's intuition is
clear from his shouting 'Nuts!' when Simon stammers 'maybe it's only

us'. Piggy can allow that one person may induce fear in another by threatening violence. This is only to allow that bullies like Jack exist. What he cannot even begin to grasp is that they may *all* be flawed by fears that lie too deep for reason to inspect and control. Such fears are beyond rational cure - ironically enough, like Piggy's asthma, with which they are causally connected. When Ralph asks Simon why he did not deny the beast's existence, he only exposes how limited in understanding he is.

By the end of the chapter we see that Ralph is involuntarily losing the leadership to Jack, and Piggy baldly states what Ralph, in his easygoing, liberal way, has not seen: that Jack hates him. Ralph, Piggy and Simon talk in the dark, 'striving unsuccessfully to convey the majesty of adult life'; but there is heavy irony here. The adult world, especially the world guaranteed by Piggy's science, is a world still more ruinous than the island, could they but know it. Meanwhile, Percival, six years old, is tortured by nightmares. He has forgotten his telephone number, but not yet his address. Not that this matters, when there are no more addresses to go to!

Chapter 6

Summary
High above the island, in the dead of night, there is an air battle, and a 'sign' from the adult world comes in the form of a dead parachutist, who is borne to the hilltop by the wind. There, as the parachute lines tauten and slacken in the breeze, the entangled body repeatedly straightens up and slumps. Sam and Eric have slept while on duty at the fire, and wake shortly before daylight. The fire is nearly out and they snigger at escaping Ralph's schoolmasterly anger; then, as they get it going properly, its light reveals the obscure figure of the dead airman. They hear the 'plopping noise' of the breeze in the parachute, clutch one another in terror, and rush down the hill to the shelters, to rouse Ralph from dreams of home.

Their story frightens Piggy as well as Ralph, who at dawn calls another assembly by passing the word around, since sounding the conch might attract the Beast. Eric takes the conch, and the twins vividly describe a Beast which they say has pursued them from the mountain top. The description horrifies the boys, but Jack proposes hunting the Beast. Though Ralph has misgivings, he takes charge of the hunt to prove he is not a coward, as Jack sneeringly suggests. He decides to leave Piggy in charge of the littluns, to Jack's open disgust. In a hostile exchange, Jack shouts at Ralph that they have no need of the conch, but Ralph, enraged, comes out best in this encounter. Though Jack backs down and Ralph wins support by talking of rescue, the conflict between them is so intense that Piggy has an attack of asthma.

The only part of the island unexplored by Jack is the tail-end, and Ralph decides they should hunt the Beast there before seeing to the fire. The biguns set out. Ralph lets Jack lead, while he keeps up the rear. Simon suspects there is no Beast, and regrets that his intuitions leave him tongue-tied. He stays close to Ralph, who badly needs support, but in his dreamy way walks into a tree. Reaching the end of the island they name the 'Castle' because it resembles a fortress, the boys pause at the narrow strip of land leading to it, and Ralph decides, as chief, to cross it, while the rest hide. Simon mumbles his disbelief in a Beast, and Ralph politely agrees, before forcing himself forward. Frightened, he looks down and sees the surge and ebb of the sea below. Suddenly realising he does not expect to find a Beast, he progresses along a ledge and reaches the Castle itself. There is no sign of a Beast. Jack joins him, and is excited by the place's potential as a fort, though Ralph sees it as 'a rotten place'. Together, they explore the Castle and for a moment recall their first happy exploration together. Jack is fascinated by the rocks, which can be tumbled into the sea, far below, while Ralph looks regretfully to where the signal fire should be burning.

The others have now crossed to the Castle. They even forget the Beast in their hooligan enthusiasm for toppling rocks into the sea, and Ralph, angry with them, tells them they must climb the mountain and renew the fire. Roger challenges this order and in the reassuring daylight the others, too, threaten to rebel. It takes all Ralph's authority to make them do as he says.

Commentary

The irony that ends the previous chapter is carried forward into the opening of this. Ralph, Piggy and Simon have pleaded for a 'sign' from what they falsely see as 'the majesty of adult life', and the fulfilment of their wish brings fresh horror into their lives. The dead parachutist becomes the Beast from Air. But a further irony is involved, since it is clear that such adults as have survived the atomic war, far from embodying majesty, are relentlessly destroying one another still. Whatever force is driving the boys on the island to self-destruction is more than paralleled in the adult world at large. Golding himself has commented that the dead airman, riddled with bullets, is an image of history; a reminder of man's unremitting aggression against man.

Though apparently animated by the wind (the tightening and slackening parachute lines are like puppet-strings), the airman's corpse is harmless; but in the uncertain light of the fire, it becomes in the twins' imagination a winged monster, all teeth and claws, that pursues them down the mountain. Their own fear projects onto it a horror that it does not have in itself, and it is precisely this horror that communicates so quickly to the other boys. Even Ralph, who significantly is woken from pleasant dreams of home, is frightened, and for all his brave words about life being scientific, Piggy's terror brings on a bad asthma attack. Ralph does not lose his sense of priorities – the fire is his first concern – but he has to compromise to retain his leadership, and instead of climbing to the fire, where the Beast was seen, he authorises the expedition to the Castle. Only Simon senses the 'personal hell' he is living through because of his inability to straighten things out and his recognition that the more talk there is about a Beast, the more they will all degenerate into animals and savages, as Piggy suggests in Chapter 5; and Simon alone offers Ralph comfort, declaring his disbelief in a Beast. What Simon *does* uniquely perceive is 'the picture of a human at once heroic and sick'. The words 'a human' here can stand for humanity, engaged in a heroic struggle that is suicidal, or specifically relate to Jack, who is brave, but sick with the lust for power.

The struggle for leadership continues. Despite Piggy's warning that Jack hates him, Ralph treats Jack with respect, seeking his opinion and even allowing him to lead the way to the Castle. But he asserts his leadership by insisting that he should cross to the Castle first and alone. Doing so, he loses any immediate sense of the danger of a Beast in his awed response to the ocean swell, and Golding, by alluding to 'a matter of centuries' that will cut off the Castle from the island, puts the action and our merely human sense of time into the vast perspective of geological time. Typically, Jack is at Ralph's heels, disobeying orders and refusing to be outdone in anything. Both boys fleetingly recall their initial comradeship on the island, but the widening gulf between them is apparent from Ralph's concern about the fire, and Jack's excitement at the idea of a fort. The remaining biguns swarm across the neck of land and share Jack's excitement, not Ralph's concern. Their primitive enjoyment of rolling rocks into the sea recalls a similar incident in Chapter 1, but points forward to the violence of Chapter 11, where Piggy will be deliberately killed by a rock toppled from the fort. Ralph is infuriated by the mindlessness of the biguns, but fails to enlist Jack's help, even when he tries to bribe him with the promise that he can lead the way to the mountain. Finally, he repeats his claim to be chief, but it is spoken to boys who are muttering mutiny, and his hold on them is at best only weak.

Chapter 7

Summary

The boys make their way to the mountain on the unfriendly side of the island, with Jack at their head. They stop to eat fruit in the heat of the day and Ralph broods on how dirty and ragged they all are. He day-dreams of a bath and haircut, and watches the heaving of the vast, alien ocean that seems to destroy all hope of rescue. Simon, intuitive as ever, tries to comfort him by telling him he will get back to his home.

Roger finds recent pig droppings and Jack takes charge of a hunt. In the middle of another daydream, Ralph is startled when a boar breaks cover, scattering the hunters. He throws his sharpened stick at it, hitting its snout, and it plunges back among the bushes and makes off. Excited by the hunt and his part in it, Ralph is boastful, but Jack, who has been slightly wounded by the boar's tusks, belittles his achievement. Further talk about what happened is accompanied by a re-enactment, with Robert playing the boar, but the game gets out of hand and Robert is lucky not to be badly injured or even killed.

They press on towards the mountain, making difficult progress because of the rocks, and at last are brought to a halt by a cliff. It is late afternoon and Ralph realises that Piggy and the littluns should not be left on their own all night. Simon, who does not fear the forest as the others do, volunteers to cross the island to join Piggy, and soon Jack is antagonising Ralph with taunts of being scared to climb the mountain. Though it is against his better judgement, Ralph follows Jack up the hillside, and Roger joins them. They cross the burnt patch, made by the forest fire, and Ralph points out that what they are doing is futile, only to meet with fresh taunts of cowardice from Jack, who goes ahead alone. It is dark, and presently Jack slithers back, badly shaken, with a report about a Beast that bulges. Ralph coolly decides they should go and look, and leads the way. As they near the top, Jack stays in the rear. Groping forward, Ralph puts his hand in the ashes of the dead signal fire, and the unexpected sensation makes him sick and dizzy. Then in the dark, they discern the large, ape-like figure of the dead, helmeted airman and glimpse 'the ruin of a face'. In panic, they hurtle back down the mountainside.

Commentary

Ralph's daydreaming relates to the disgust and self-disgust he feels at the outward deterioration of the boys from middle-class standards: a deterioration that has an *inward* equivalent, as he well knows. His day-dreams reveal Ralph as typically middle-class in background. He is the son of a naval officer, used to the comfort and security of a good home, with special bedtime treats, and books of his own, which – ironically, considering he is now tracking a Beast – used to frighten him with the picture of a spider. His yearning for home is so strong, he can almost evoke the physical sensation of its reassuring objects.

The boar explodes into this world of daydreams, and Ralph has nerve enough to stand his ground and hurl his stick at it. More importantly, he is exhilarated by the wild excitement of this – an excitement that enables him to identify with the hunters – and within minutes of daydreaming about 'bright copper kettles' and the warm comfort of home, he is part of the savage 'game' in which he grabs murderously at the 'brown, vulnerable flesh' of Robert, who has to struggle frenziedly to avoid being killed. We should note how Golding creates some of his most powerful effects by cumulative repetition. In Chapter 5, Maurice distracts the frightened littluns by clowning the part of a pig in a mock hunt; then the chapter closes with the foreboding ritualising of a hunt. Here, the savagery nearly leads to a death, and Jack makes a black joke about using a littlun as a pig. In Chapter 9, the ritual will claim Simon as a sacrifice.

The rivalry between Ralph and Jack continues to become still more bitter in this chapter. Jack's loathing of Piggy, who has asthma and cannot hunt, is so great that it strangles his voice: he cannot bear Ralph's respect for a fat weakling, he has no sympathy for the littluns, and his sneers and taunts arise from this. Ralph for the first time realises how violently Jack resents him, but by openly asking Jack to say why he hates him, Ralph breaks a schoolboy taboo and embarrasses the biguns. As the bitterness between the rivals intensifies, their exchanges become icily casual:

'If you don't mind, of course.'
'Oh, not at all.'

It is odd to think that the topic is a terrifying Beast, but the conversational clichés of their class are powerfully charged here. By rising to Jack's baiting, Ralph is compelled to act against his better judgement, which weakens what authority he still has. In the battle of wills between them, each one seeks to score over the other, and we should note how first one, then the other, leads the biguns, and finally the expedition to the mountain top. For the first time ever, we see Jack hesitate when Ralph, hearing his story about the Beast, coolly proposes they go and investigate. Ralph surprises himself by such bravado, but he is inwardly terrified, seeming to hear Piggy's accusation that he is acting like a kid. When his hand is unexpectedly thrust into the cold ash of the dead fire, his fear is so overwhelming that it affects his sense of balance, so that the mountain seems to slide sideways, and the physical world ceases to be real.

Chapter 8

Summary
As the dawn breaks, Ralph gives an exaggerated account of the Beast to Piggy. Jack takes offence when Ralph insults his hunters, and calls an assembly in which he denounces Ralph, accusing him of being a coward and no more a 'proper chief' than Piggy is. He fails in his attempt to get the boys to vote against Ralph's continuing to be chief, and in deep humiliation declares he will no longer 'be part of Ralph's lot'; then goes angrily off on his own, though he invites his hunters to join him. Piggy is confident they can get by without Jack. Ralph believes Jack will return when it is dark, but feels despondent. Simon, amid muted jeers, struggles to say they ought to climb the mountain, but his suggestion is ignored. Piggy, however, startles the boys with a suggestion that they should light a signal fire near the beach, away from the Beast, and soon the boys set about gathering wood. For the first time, Piggy himself lights the fire with the lens of his spectacles, and is beginning to apply his practical intelligence to its maintenance, when Ralph notices that several of the hunters are missing. They have slunk away to join Jack. Ralph gives way to dejection, and Piggy and the twins bring a feast of fruit to cheer him. Meanwhile, Simon has withdrawn to his hiding place in the forest.

Jack is triumphant when he is joined by boys who desert Ralph, and appoints himself chief. They are to forget the Beast, he tells his followers; they will kill a pig and hold a feast, and make a fort of the Castle Rock. Jack creeps up on a herd of pigs and signals to the rest that they are to attack a large sow, which they impale with spears, track down and kill with extreme violence in a clearing in the forest. Jack rubs the sow's blood on Maurice's face. The boys are sadistically delighted to discover that Roger has forced his spear up the sow's 'ass'. Jack orders a feast to be prepared further along the beach; but before they go, they sharpen a stick at both ends and ram it in the earth, with the pig's head stuck at its other end, as a gift to the Beast. Then, awed by what they have done, they run away, half in panic.

From his hideout, Simon has witnessed the kill, and as he gazes fascinated at the pig's head, he enters into an hallucinatory conversation with it. The spiked head tells him that things are bad; that he should run away; that the whole thing is a joke and not worth bothering about. An oppressive heat is building up to a storm, and as Simon watches the pig's head and the flies that swarm around it and around himself, he feels in his temple a pulsing that heralds an epileptic fit.

As the thunder begins, Ralph confesses to Piggy that he is scared, not simply of the heat, but of the way in which, with reduced numbers, the fire cannot be kept going. Rescue seems impossible. The others do not care, and sometimes he ceases to care himself: moreover, he cannot understand what it is that ruins everything they try to do. Piggy, happy to be Ralph's confidant, blames Jack. Their talk is shattered by an invasion of Jack and four of his hunters, all painted, who steal fire. Jack pauses to tell Ralph and his followers that he *may* let them join his tribe, and invites them to the feast he is giving. Urged on by Jack, his savages declare: 'The Chief has spoken'. Ralph talks to his followers about how important the fire is, but his mind is so distraught he cannot say why, and Piggy has to prompt him with the word 'rescue'. Meanwhile, all Ralph's group, including Piggy, are sorely tempted by the thought of meat.

Simon continues to confront the pig's head. He will not run away, as it seems to command, and he rejects the suggestion that it is a Beast. It claims it is part of him, the reason for all that is bad, and warns him he had better join the others, or be killed for not doing so. Simon pitches forward in a fit.

Commentary

Ralph's description of the Beast is a wild distortion and another instance of the theme concerning what is real and what unreal. Throughout the novel, Golding shows us things not as they might appear to a neutral observer, but as they are coloured and shaped by the hopes, fears and other emotions of the boys themselves. The thing that squats by the fire is not only exaggerated into a bogey with frightening teeth and eyes: as Ralph sees it, superstitiously, it also opposes the possibility of rescue. Jack makes exaggerated claims for his hunters, and Ralph's realism in replying leads to Jack's mutiny; but just as Ralph sees the Beast as opposing rescue (which is his overriding concern), so Jack sees it as a hunter (which betrays his own obsession).

Jack's challenge for the leadership involves him in denouncing Ralph as a talker, like Piggy, and not a hunter, who can supply meat. In Chapter 1, Jack staked a claim to leadership by appealing to schoolboy standards, but ever since he has ignored them, until now, when he surprisingly and incongruously dredges up the charge that Ralph 'isn't a prefect'. But Jack miscalculates when he asks the boys to vote against Ralph. Their silence and embarrassment torment and enrage him, and in his humiliation he falls back on a child's idiom, declaring he will no longer 'play'. The word has unmistakable echoes of a school playground, but at the same time betrays Jack's vision of life on the island. Later, when the deserters join him, making him 'brilliantly happy', Jack elaborates the 'play' element in their lives by insisting on the use of the ritual formula, 'The Chief has spoken'; but just how murderous 'play' as

Jack understands it can become is brought home to us by the killing of the sow. Though they are too ashamed openly to vote against Ralph, the biguns who desert are attracted precisely by the 'play' Jack offers them. Hunting and eating pig are more dramatic and adventurous activities, particularly to young boys, than building shelters, tending a fire and eating insipid fruit can ever be.

Ralph's despair incapacitates what small leadership he has left, after the desertion, and Piggy, knowing that no one will accept his own leadership, has to prompt Ralph even about their first priority: 'I could tell you what Ralph's going to say next. The most important thing. . . is the smoke. . .'. And later, when Ralph's brain is clouded, Piggy has to remind him of the connection between the fire and rescue. Ralph is beginning to crack under the strain; he cannot grasp why things are falling apart; he can no longer think straight, and is increasingly dependent on Piggy.

Jack celebrates his chieftainship by leading his hunters to a killing that is deliberately described in sexual terms, so that the boys, though they have not reached puberty, seem degraded and defiled by the anal rape they commit. They are 'wedded' to the sow 'in lust'; the air is 'full of sweat and noise and blood and terror'; Roger finds 'lodgment for his point', while hot blood spouts all over Jack's hands; and finally, with the sow collapsed under them, they lie 'heavy and fulfilled upon her'. With such images clinging to them, the boys' innocence, such as it was, is finally destroyed.

Unable to get a hearing when he suggests they should climb the mountain and squarely face the Beast, Simon has retreated to his hide-out near the clearing; but instead of finding peace there, and enjoyment of nature's delicate beauty, symbolised in the butterflies, he is witness to the bloodlust of the hunters in their rape-murder of the sow. When the hunters escape in shame and fear, he is left with the spiked pig's head, the spilled entrails and the swarm of flies. The oppressive heat, building up to the thunderstorm, matches the rising tension in the boy, as he senses the onset of an epileptic fit, and hears the hallucinatory voice of the Lord of the Flies, as the pig's head is called. We have reached a point at the very heart of the novel. The half-shut eyes of the spiked head are 'dim with the infinite cynicism of adult life', and assure Simon that 'everything is a bad business'. But Simon knows both the cynicism of the adult world (indeed, he is mocked even in a child's world), and the nature of evil itself. We are again confronted by the paradoxical nature of reality. Simon hears a schoolmaster's voice and sees a grotesquely ballooning head in his hallucination. But he holds on to what he knows inside him is true and real. The voice may explain things away, or belittle him, or urge him to join the rest and be as they are, believing in a Beast. Simon, physically ill, stands his ground and affirms the truth: the Lord of the Flies is 'Pig's head on a stick'. No more. He resists the temptation to be like the others, and so avoid accusations of being 'batty'. He knows that things fall apart and break up because of the evil inherent in all human beings; as a result of 'mankind's essential sickness'. Not even the threat of death can deflect him from the certainty of this.

Chapter 9

Summary
As he passes into a fit, Simon has a nosebleed, and sleeps until evening, while the storm gathers over the island. Waking, he hauls himself from the earth by means of the creepers, disturbing the flies that infest the guts of the pig. In the strange twilight he asks aloud, 'What else is there to do?' and with painful effort makes his way through the forest to climb the mountain. He sees something humped on the top, but keeps climbing still, hiding his face. Finally, crawling, he discovers the airman's corpse as it twitches back and forth, pulled by the parachute strings as the wind plays in the parachute. Inside the helmet, the face is decomposing, and the flies swarm around it. Simon vomits, then frees the entangled lines. Far below, he can see smoke and the figures of boys on the beach, and he staggers down the mountain to tell them the Beast is harmless.

Ralph and Piggy bathe in the oppressive heat. A few littluns remain with them, but the biguns have joined Jack's feast. Piggy suggests they should do so, too, overtly to ensure no mischief occurs. As they approach, they hear the noise of a party and see Jack wearing a garland and presiding. Silence falls on the boys and Ralph and Piggy affect indifference as they stroll by, but Piggy is bumped into by the cooks, who are hauling roast pig, and is burnt. The tension is snapped. Everybody is relieved by Piggy's misfortune, and Jack orders meat to be given to the intruders, who take it, dribbling. Jack asks if everybody has eaten his fill and commands everybody to sit. Ralph and Piggy continue to stand as Jack, speaking from his log-throne, asks who will join his tribe, to be given meat and protection from the Beast. Ralph declares that he is chief, and speaks about a signal fire, and the authority of the conch, which Jack rejects. As the storm begins to break, Piggy tries to get Ralph to leave, but Ralph scores over Jack by asking where his shelters are. For answer, Jack calls on everyone to dance and, with Roger as pig, they begin to form a circle, carrying spears and clubs, and chanting. Ralph and Piggy cannot resist joining in the communal frenzy. Roger leaves the circle, which opens out into a horseshoe, into which Simon crawls, exhausted and trying to say what the Beast really is. He breaks out of the ring, but the crowd follows, then closes in and beats and tears him till he is dead, under the downpour of rain.

A powerful wind fills and carries the parachute with its dead airman from the mountain top into the open sea. Simon's body is claimed by the tide's swell and borne out to sea under a sky that has cleared and is bright with stars.

Commentary

The chapter's title, 'A View to a Death', is taken from the famous song, 'John Peel'. Golding begins and ends the chapter with powerful descriptive passages. The opening describes the stifling, ominous build-up of a tropical storm, but it is a build-up that parallels the rising tension of the action, the climax of which is matched by the heaven's explosion and the downpour of rain. There is a hint of a parallel, too, between Simon's nosebleed and the storm's release, as if to reflect the difference in scale between the miniscule human world and the stupendous world of the elements, a theme elaborated in the chapter's conclusion.

Simon's exhausting climb to the mountain top (a struggle to reach the truth) is made because he refuses to take the easy way and identify with the others. He has an unfailing intuition that approaches visionary revelation, and he remains faithful to it, whatever the cost. Ironically, this is seen by the others as 'battiness'. His discovery of the dead airman confirms his disbelief in a Beast, and after compassionately releasing the parachute strings, his first thought is to tell the others and so relieve them of fear. He struggles heroically and self-sacrificingly (literally so) to share his discovery, only to be torn apart by those he seeks to save. His murderers make a scapegoat of him, and in their mass madness treat him as a Beast, unaware that what they are really doing is to project onto him their own fear and bestiality.

We should note that Ralph and, more particularly, Piggy are drawn to the feast by their greed for meat, however Piggy might rationalise their action. The boy Jack, now transformed into a tribal chief and enthroned 'like an idol', has apparently won the long tug-of-war with Ralph for leadership. He is less an individual than an embodiment of power and authority: but his power resides in 'the brown swell of his forearms' and is physical, while his authority sits on his shoulders and chatters 'like an ape', because it is savage and animal. Piggy's questions – 'What are we? Humans? Or animals? Or savages' (Chapter 5) – seem to be finally answered. Then the onset of the storm gives Ralph a temporary advantage, since Jack can provide no shelter, and the littluns hurtle around, screaming with fear; but the advantage is short-lived. Jack evades Ralph's challenge by commanding the dance which obliterates personal identity among the dancers. Even Ralph and Piggy surrender to the pulse of the chant and become part of 'the throb and stamp of a single organism' that destroys Simon.

The conclusion of the chapter is a sustained and sublime celebration of beauty, both as it appears in the minute 'moonbeam-bodied creatures' that lap around the pathetic, huddled body of Simon, and in the majesty of the distant constellations. The dead airman returns to the ocean, a symbol of eternity. So, too, does Simon, who loved nature, and whose body is assimilated to its majestic processes.

Chapter 10

Summary

Ralph, dirty and damaged from taking part in the frenzied dancing of the previous evening, joins Piggy on the platform where once assemblies were held. All the biguns except Piggy and the twins, Sam and Eric, have gone over to Jack; a few littluns remain. Ralph insists on talking about Simon, and Piggy, extremely uneasy, comes up with all sorts of excuses: it was dark; it was the dance; they were scared; perhaps Simon is only pretending to be dead; they were on the outside of the circle; it was an accident, and Simon's own fault. Ralph knows these are evasions; he cannot bear to be touched by Piggy, or settle for Piggy's solution to the problem, which is to conceal the fact that they took part in the dance. They are joined by Sam and Eric, who are dragging a log to the fire, and whose guilt for their own part in the dance is betrayed by their haste in explaining that they 'got lost last night'. Piggy explains that Ralph and he left early, after the feast, and Sam and Eric claim to have done the same; but they all know in their hearts that this is an unconvincing 'cover up'.

Castle Rock has been made into a fort by Jack. It is guarded by a sentry able to topple a rock on an approaching enemy. Robert and Roger talk of Jack as 'a proper Chief', who has power to beat a savage, apparently for nothing. This excites Roger, a sadist with a lust for 'irresponsible authority'. Jack is now always addressed as Chief, and gives orders arbitrarily from behind his mask of paint. He wants his sentries to stop all comers to the fort, including the Beast. A savage hesitantly suggests that they have killed the Beast, and they all remember the dance; but the Chief declares that it cannot be killed, that it comes in disguise, and that it should be kept at bay by being given part of their kill. The Chief ordains a feast next day, and plans to solve the problem of how to make a fire.

Along the beach, Ralph, Piggy, Sam and Eric huddle for comfort round the signal fire, which because there are so few of them it is difficult to keep fed, and Ralph has to be prompted again by Piggy to make the link between the fire and rescue. They allow the fire to go out overnight, since they are too frightened to gather wood in the dark, and go to a shelter to sleep. Ralph dreams of rescue and security, the twins share a nightmare, and in the dark Ralph and Piggy whisper about the need to get home before they all go mad. Then they hear movements outside and feel panic, thinking it is the Beast. Piggy suffers an asthma attack. In the dark, Jack, Roger and Maurice suddenly attack, and a chaotic struggle follows, in which Ralph and Eric unknowingly fight one another. The shelter collapses and the raiders make off. The conch is untouched, but they have taken Piggy's spectacles, and are jubilant with success.

Commentary
Ralph faces squarely Simon's murder and his own part in it. Piggy protests shrilly because he cannot admit his guilt. Ralph laughs hysterically, and recognises, even in the agony of his guilt, the fascination of evil: his 'loathing' is also a 'feverish excitement'. None of this is acknowledged by Piggy, who dishonestly searches for a 'formula' that exempts them from all blame, and even suggests Simon 'asked for it', so pinning the blame onto the blameless (though imprudent) victim. There is a hint that Ralph has a glimpse of Simon's vision when he says: 'I'm frightened. Of us.' But Piggy is both self-deceiving, insisting it was all 'an accident', and intent on deceiving others: 'don't let on we was at that dance'. If we are invited to admire Piggy's intellect on some occasions in the story, we are just as certainly asked to condemn it here, and to contrast his 'We never done nothing, we never seen nothing' with Simon's heroic determination to climb the mountain and reveal the truth. The author's irony is never more concentrated than when he speaks of Ralph, Piggy and the twins all shaking convulsively as they remember 'the dance that none of them attended'.

   At Castle Rock, the boy Jack is now forgotten in the Chief, just as his features are lost behind the mask of paint. His arbitrary exercise of power over his 'savages' stimulates the sadistic impulse in Roger, who shares his Chief's preoccupation with destruction. Though secure in his Chieftainship, Jack has to quell the unease and doubts of his savages, who also remember Simon's murder with a sense of guilt. He finds an explanation that involves the kind of 'double-think' practised by those who are in the grip of fear and superstition, arguing that the Beast takes on different disguises and therefore can never be finally killed. His savages accept whatever he says, partly from fear of him, partly because, like Piggy, they cannot face the truth and are willing to flinch away from memories that are too painful to bear, even if doing so involves

the rejection of rationality. When the Chief has a 'theological specula-
tion', he senses the need to placate the Beast with a sacrificial offering,
and implicitly sees it as supernatural.

Ralph's daydreaming, or game of 'supposing', focuses on home. His
mental blackouts are worsening and he is tormented by guilt, so that
not surprisingly his 'supposing' offers an escape from harsh reality. But
now, even Dartmoor's wildness disturbs him, and he diverts his daydreaming to 'a tamed town' and the safety of a bus station. But this
affords him no escape, for it turns into a nightmare when a strange bus
crawls out of the bus station, and we realise, though it is not said, that
this is linked emotionally with Simon's crawling out of the feast.

In the last paragraph, the reference to phosphorescence reminds us
that the beach where the savages exultingly turn cartwheels to celebrate
their success in stealing Piggy's spectacles is the same beach on which
Simon's body lay huddled. Meanwhile, Piggy, the intellectual, and guide
and friend to Ralph, is now virtually blind and incapacitated.

Chapter 11

Summary
Ralph, Piggy and the twins have no means of rekindling the dead signal
fire. At Piggy's suggestion, Ralph sounds the conch and a few littluns
join the four biguns for an assembly. Piggy can barely see and is in
despair. Ralph points out that they have no fire and therefore cannot
be rescued; he suggests that they should smarten themselves up and visit
Jack and his savages. Piggy has a pathetic faith in the power of the
conch, and proposes taking it to Jack, with the reproach that Jack has
stolen his spectacles and must restore them because 'What's right's right'.

The four biguns discuss how they should prepare themselves for
their visit to Castle Rock. Ralph insists that they will not paint themselves, and talks about the need for smoke, though he is not clear as to
its purpose, as the twins notice uneasily. He heads the group as they
make their way to Castle Rock, with Piggy in the rear, proudly clutching
the conch. They carry spears for their protection, and Piggy moves
uncertainly to second place behind Ralph as he crosses the neck of land
leading to Jack's fortress. Roger challenges them from a pinnacle above,
and as Ralph blows the conch, the painted savages emerge. When Ralph
announces he is calling an assembly, Roger begins to throw stones; then
Jack, returning from hunting, comes up from behind, and demands to
know what Ralph wants. The twins, frightened, move forward, to a
point between Ralph and the savages. Jack orders Ralph away, but
Ralph angrily tells him he is a thief, and must give back Piggy's spectacles. The two boys grapple and their positions on the neck of land

are reversed. There is a lull in the fight, during which Ralph appeals to a code of honour that means nothing to Jack and his savages. More talk about the fire and rescue falls on dead ears. Jack orders the capture of the twins, trapped between himself and his savages, and despite their protests they are taken and bound. Fighting resumes when Ralph tries to interpose, while Piggy crouches, fearful and unseeing.

Though they try to injure one another, Ralph and Jack are each nervous of the other, and in a further pause, Piggy holds out the conch and accuses the savages of behaving like 'kids'. He is booed, as is Ralph when he asks whether law and rescue are better than hunting and violence. Meanwhile, high above them, Roger leans on the lever that dislodges a huge rock. It strikes Piggy, whose body lands forty feet below on a slab of rock; his brains spill out and the swell of the tide sucks the body into the sea. Jack hurls his spear at Ralph, who is wounded, and as the other savages advance on him, he dashes off into the forest. The captured twins are submitted to torture at the hands of Roger.

Commentary

The chapter recounts the total defeat of Ralph's group. From the first, there is pathos in their small numbers, in Piggy's blindness, and in the fact that the only fire, and the only means of making fire, are with Jack and his savages, who care nothing about rescue. Similarly pathetic is the assembly, a mere token of earlier, larger assemblies that have left their impress on the trodden grass. Piggy is reduced to snivelling about the 'awful things' that have been done, and on this occasion he refers directly to Simon's murder. It is Ralph who cannot bring himself to do so. But both Ralph and Piggy share a sense of moral outrage, and both cling to the belief that they can still appeal to the better nature of Jack and his savages. Ralph deludes himself with the thought that if he, Piggy and the twins conform to previously respected standards by washing and generally tidying themselves, this will induce a sense of shame in the savages. Just as unrealistically, Piggy thinks that the savages will continue to respect the conch's authority, and will succumb to his moral appeal that they should do what is right for its own sake. Meanwhile, the alert reader notices how the conch is forebodingly described as 'fragile'. This helps to prepare us for the tragedy that follows.

Signs are also given us that the twins, Sam and Eric, cannot be wholly relied on. They live in fear of Jack and are tempted to imitate him by painting themselves, though Ralph stamps firmly on their suggestion; and when Ralph comes near to quarrelling hysterically with Piggy, insisting that he never forgets the purpose of the smoke, they are puzzled by a strange weakness in a leader they had always believed to be solid and reliable. Ralph is visibly losing his grip on things, and with it, his authority.

As the boys make their way to Castle Rock, a sense of unreality is created by the heat haze, the mirages and the slightly sinister 'plate-like shadows' that they themselves cast on a beach still littered with the debris of the tribe's murderous dance. Groping blindly behind Ralph, Piggy has a terrifying intuition of danger, and cringes on the narrow path, forty feet above the altar-like slab of rock on to which he will later fall, like a sacrifice. When Ralph tries to call an assembly, there is an unresponsive silence. Then Roger, as if recapitulating the action of Chapter 4, in which he threw stones to miss Henry, pelts Ralph with stones still aimed to miss; but here, as always in the novel's develop-ment, there is an intensification of what has gone before, as 'some source of power' begins to 'pulse in Roger's body', destroying restraint. It is with 'delirious abandonment' that he leans all his weight on the lever that topples the great boulder by which Piggy is struck down. Roger, a born sadist, realises his true nature in unbridled violence, enjoying the 'hangman's horror' that clings to him. His need to torture Sam and Eric is so overpowering that he all but nudges Jack aside, in his haste to get at them.

Piggy's destruction appropriately coincides with the shattering into smithereens of the conch he reveres because of the values it stands for: free and democratic speech, an adult sense of responsibility, law and order. When Piggy dies, these values die, too. Piggy's death is, in fact, the brutal answer given by Jack and his savages to Piggy's and Ralph's appeal to their sense of decency, fair-play and honour. Discussion and reason and argument are at an end. Violence and assertion through force and murder are all that are left. Confronted with the painted mask of the Chief, Ralph has to struggle to remember what the boy Jack had looked like. Savagery has destroyed individual identity. There is something ludicrous about Ralph's reproaches and the twins' expostu-lations: the very words they use are middle-class clichés that might carry weight on the playing fields of Eton, but are grotesquely out of place on Castle Rock, significantly the harshest and most primitive part of the island. It is now Jack's capital, from which, with absolute auth-ority, he imposes his rule of terror.

Chapter 12

Summary
Ralph, wounded, hides in dense forest growth until evening, then under cover of darkness creeps to Castle Rock, where the savages are roasting a pig. Robert is on guard. Hungry, Ralph finds fruit to eat near the

shelters, and terrifies two littluns by his battered appearance. He limps back towards the enemy camp, trying to persuade himself that the others cannot be as bad as in his heart he knows them to be, and finds himself face to face with the spiked pig's head in the clearing. It disgusts him, and he flays out at it with his fists, dislodging it from its stick, which he seizes as a spear before backing off and reapproaching Castle Rock. The tribe there are feasting and chanting, and Ralph can hardly resist the temptation to join them; but 'darkness and the horrors of death' prevent him. Coming still closer, he detects the twins keeping guard and clambers towards them, whispering. They cling to one another in fear, then Sam tries to do his duty, telling Ralph to go away, warning him of the danger he is in and of how he will be hunted like a pig next day. Ralph is delirious with fear and hunger: the sky seems to lurch around him, and beneath him the sea sucks at the rock that claimed Piggy. Sam and Eric speak of the Chief and Roger as 'terrors'; they are too frightened to join Ralph, though they thrust meat into his hands as he scrambles away. When he pleads with them to know what the tribe will do to him, all they dare whisper is that Roger has sharpened a stick at both ends. Ralph fails to grasp what this means.

Having told the twins that he will hide in the nearby thicket, he retreats there, and broods on Piggy's death and the meaning of the stick sharpened at both ends. Noises indicate that Samneric have been suspected of aiding Ralph and are being tortured. Ralph sleeps, only to waken to the cry of the hunters, who call to each other as they close in on the thicket where he lies hidden. Under torture 'Samneric' have betrayed his hiding place, and rocks are toppled from above on to the thicket; then a savage penetrates near him, and Ralph strikes out with his spear, wounding him. The hunters set fire to the thicket to smoke him out. Ralph makes for the forest, furious as an animal, stabbing a savage that stands in his way.

Stretched out in a cordon, the savages scour the forest for Ralph, who cannot think properly, and who finds himself in the clearance where the pig's head was offered to the Beast. He plunges into the densest thicket for cover, and waits there, hearing the grumble of the fire, which is sweeping the forest. Ralph now sees the stick he holds is sharpened at both ends, and clutches it tight as a hunter kneels, peering to find him. Leaping out at the savage, Ralph runs desperately, till he reaches the shore, where he collapses, exhausted, and begging for mercy.

Staggering again to his feet, he sees a smartly dressed naval officer standing above him. The savages come forward, 'a semi-circle of little boys', now. Meanwhile, the naval officer explains that the forest fire has brought him to their rescue. He tries to joke about the boys' games, and is disturbed to find they have behaved less well than boys do in such fictions as *The Coral Island*. Ralph cries convulsively, and soon the other boys are sobbing, too, while the naval officer turns away in embarrassment, to give them time to pull themselves together.

Commentary

Ralph, at bay, cannot quite grasp the full truth of what is happening to him. He is torn by conflicting thoughts and impulses, longing to join the savages, but not daring to; dribbling with hunger, but hating the living still more. In words that recall Piggy's in Chapter 10, he tries to persuade himself that the deaths have been 'an accident', that all will be well if only he can return casually to the others; but inside himself he knows a dreadful fate awaits him, not least because of a basic respect he and Jack have for one another – a respect that paradoxically requires Jack to destroy him. And all, as he tells himself, because he has held on to sanity and 'sense', and refused to surrender his individual identity to the anonymous collective identity of the tribe.

Just how filthy, battered and bruised Ralph is can be judged from the way the two littluns scream and run off at the sight of him. We are given various clues to his physical and psychological condition. He is wounded, exhausted and constantly on the verge of hysteria. Confronted with the skull of the pig, or Lord of the Flies, he cannot, like Simon, come to terms with it, which would involve an acceptance of it as part of himself, so he lashes out in fury, trying to destroy its obscene grin. But far from succeeding, he only magnifies the obscenity, for the shattered skull's grin broadens to be 'six feet across'. Then, when he climbs the rock face to whisper furtively with 'Samneric', he is conscious of the death rock below him, and the sea that claimed Piggy, and the combination of his emotional intensity and physical weakness sets the heavens reeling, so that the stars seem to spill and dance overhead. At the same time, he feels 'the dull pain of these things', which are beyond words, and we are reminded of Simon's intuitive grasp of mankind's 'essential sickness'.

Justice has ceased to have meaning. Though Ralph can legitimately protest that he has done nothing, and 'only wanted to keep up a fire', the fact is that nothing makes sense any more. As Eric tells him: 'Never mind what's sense. That's gone – '. A rule of terror imposes its own arbitrary terms: it is about torture and power, and nothing else; least of all about justice and reason. Though Ralph is slow to understand what the stick sharpened at both ends means, we know that Roger has made a stake for Ralph's head, and since he is to be hunted like a pig, the chances are he will be eaten like one, too.

In the hunt, Ralph is himself degraded into savagery and even animality. Just as his anxieties in the past led him to bite his nails without knowing it, the terrors of the hunt now lead him to chew the bark off his spear. His teeth are exposed by his snarls, he leaps out at his enemy 'like a cat', and the curtain in his brain blacks out, leaving him with a merely instinctual awareness. As the savages and the forest fire close in on him, he sees that the stick he is clutching is sharpened at both ends; but it is uncertain whether he fully comprehends the clue. As readers, we suffer the frightening climax of the novel's action exclusively in terms that relate to Ralph. Everything is observed through his eyes: we identify with his wounds, his terror, and his panic. Finally, he bursts from the thicket like a pig, and 'screaming, snarling, bloody' runs to the beach, though he is by now so exhausted and distraught that his legs seem no longer his own. When he falls on the sand and crouches, arm raised to ward off the hunters' spears, we accept Ralph's death. It is part of the imaginative logic of the story and has all the inevitability necessary for satisfying the reader of the novel's psychological truth. In effect, this is the end of the story.

What follows surprises the reader and throws everything preceding it into a startling and new perspective. By means of the naval officer, Golding brings us abruptly back to a reality his artistic skill has enabled us almost to overlook. These are, after all, only 'little boys': Ralph is a 'little scarecrow' in need of 'a nose-wipe and a good deal of ointment'; Jack is a 'little boy' with the remnant of a black cap and 'the remains of a pair of spectacles at his waist'; the rest are 'tiny tots', one of whom, Percival Wemys Madison, cannot even remember his own name, let alone his address.

But *this* reality - reality as seen by the naval officer - is itself unreal. The adult that intrudes is more of a child than the children he patronises. He steps straight out of the pages of *The Coral Island*, which he refers to, because the book's impossibly idealised representation of children on an island corresponds exactly with his own expectations about children. Golding invests everything he says with biting irony. He cheerfully asks if they are having 'fun and games', which recalls the boys' earliest expectations; whether they are 'having a war or something', which, tragically, is exactly what they are doing; and whether there are 'any dead bodies'. The truth, when it comes out, embarrasses him; it is more than he can take, and not at all what he expects of British boys (an echo of Jack's boast that the British are best at everything). He does the decent thing by turning away, to give the boys time to stop sobbing and pull themselves together again, as story-book boys would do. But Ralph certainly, and the others perhaps, weep for 'the end of innocence, the darkness of man's heart', and in doing so are in essentials older and immeasurably more experienced than the naval officer, whose adult pose is superficial, uncomprehending and even hypocritical.

For what, after all, does rescue imply? Their own tribal war is finished, and their island devastated, but rescue can only take them into a world which is similarly devastated by an atomic war that still rages. Their rescuer lacks their first-hand experience of the 'darkness of man's heart', and is ignorant of what war and his own part in it really mean. The adult world he represents is in ruins, but his confidence is untouched because, for the moment, he is neatly uniformed, with a gun at his waist, a cutter behind him, with its ratings and sub-machine gun at the alert, and behind that, in the distance, the 'trim cruiser' – 'trim' because ready for action. The adult world is, in fact, a kind of macrocosm of the small island, a projection on to a vastly larger screen of the fears, superstitions, hatreds and murderous violence of the boys who have reduced their island to a charred and sterile waste. Though the naval officer is physically adult, he is too shallow and naïve to understand the tragic pain felt by the semicircle of small boys who, contrary to the best traditions about keeping a stiff upper lip, let the side down by openly weeping.

If the device of the naval officer gives a whole new perspective to the children's world, the children just as surely afford the reader a whole new perspective on the adult world.

4 THEMES

4.1 DISEASED AND FALLEN HUMAN NATURE

The theme of mankind's diseased and fallen nature is the central theme of the novel, and extends pervasively to such other themes as fear and power. In deciding to make his boys real, Golding was consciously challenging the idealised characters of *The Coral Island*, who are portrayed as unselfish, courageous and mindful of both their Creator and their beloved parents. In sharp contrast to Ballantyne's boys, who work in loving co-operation for the common good, without so much as an impure word, thought or deed, Golding's boys are shown to be selfish, greedy, superstitiously afraid, unmindful of their Creator, and forgetful of their parents and the standards imposed by adult authority. They are, moreover, cruel, uncooperative, vindictive and finally self-destructive.

We may in part explain such radically opposed views about what boys are like by examining the historical contexts in which *The Coral Island* and *Lord of the Flies* were written. R. M. Ballantyne wrote in 1858, in a world that was becoming increasingly dominated by European technology, culture and religion. Britain in particular controlled a vast empire, and the British confidently believed they had a God-given right to extend to the rest of the world the material benefits of a progress for which they took much of the credit. The future appeared to hold out the hope of a still greater prosperity and unlimited progress. But a century later, when Golding wrote his fable, such optimistic Victorian hopes had been very thoroughly discredited. Industrial depression, the breaking up of the British Empire, the decline of religion, and two world wars, ending in the horrors of the concentration camps and the dropping of atomic bombs on Hiroshima and Nagasaki, destroyed all faith in 'progress' for Golding and many of his generation, and his island fable can be thought of as expressing the disillusioned pessimism of the 1950s.

Though this approach has value and is probably enough to explain Ballantyne, it fails to do justice to Golding, who has always had a preoccupation with ancient civilisations and with pre-history (his second novel, *The Inheritors*, is about Neanderthal Man's encounter with Homo Sapiens). In *Lord of the Flies* Golding is clearly seeking to explore fundamental human nature, and this is apparent from the way in which he portrays the slackening hold of civilisation on the boys and their consequent atavistic regression. By reversing mankind's evolution and abbreviating time, he strips his boys to their essential nature, which is shown to be one of murderous savagery.

In doing this, there can be little doubt that Golding is inverting not simply Ballantyne's idealisation, but the whole Romantic tradition of 'the noble savage'. According to this tradition, which stems from the French philosopher Jean Jacques Rousseau, man's basic nature is good, but it has been corrupted by civilisation and perverted by Society's political, religious, educational and legal institutions from its pristine innocence and goodness. This belief is akin to the numerous utopian myths that tell of a golden world set in the past – Atlantis or Arcadia or Eden itself. At an opposite extreme to this utopianism affirming man's essential natural goodness, is the belief that man is by nature essentially sinful. One powerful assertion of this within Christian tradition is the doctrine of original sin, associated with St Augustine (345-430 AD). This holds that human nature is so fundamentally bad that it can be redeemed only through divine grace, never through man's own unaided efforts. It is a profoundly pessimistic belief, and one that Golding apparently accepts. 'Man,' he tells us, 'is a fallen being. He is gripped by original sin' (*The Hot Gates*, 1965).

Even so, we must distinguish between what Golding asserts here and what the novel itself actually conveys. What it does *not* specifically convey is 'original sin' in the Augustinian sense. There is no overt religious, let alone Christian, testimony in the novel. At best, we can say it portrays 'original sin' only if we use the term loosely, as an equivalent to an ingrained and ineradicable flaw in human nature. It is through Simon's 'ancient, inescapable recognition' that we, as readers, are made aware of mankind's evil – his 'essential sickness'; but here again, we should be on our guard when Golding calls Simon a 'saint', since the word has no specifically Christian reference, however convenient it may be as a metaphor.

Lord of the Flies works on the principle of exposing the inherent evil in its characters gradually and through ironic repetitions of behaviour (see Section 4.3). Jack turns into an arbitrarily cruel tribal chief who orders Ralph's death at the hands of his choirboys, who have themselves turned into merciless savages; Roger becomes a torturer, driven by

sadistic lust; the innocence of make-believe and 'fun and games' degen-
erates into savagery and the murderous assault on Simon. But the point
is not that these things happen, but that they represent the realisation
of the characters' instincts and the fulfilment of their most basic, and
therefore most authentic, selves.

Nor can it be argued that at least some characters escape the 'essential illness' of human evil. If it is truly 'essential', it must exist in every
human being, and it is in fact shown to afflict all Golding's boys. This is
not to deny that Ralph, Piggy and Simon are capable of good inten-
tions and actions. Clearly they are; but deep within them all is an evil
they share with Jack and Roger. When Robert is acting the pig in game,
Ralph as well as Roger fights to get close, trying 'to get a handful of
that vulnerable flesh. The desire to squeeze and hurt was overmastering'
(Chapter 7). All the boys, in varying degrees, fear the Beast, just as all
of them, Piggy included, become part of 'a single organism' and destroy
Simon in a murderous frenzy. That is the outlet for their own bestiality
(see *Specimen Passage*, pp. 77–82).

The only character never shown to be involved in evil is Simon,
whose most reprehensible act is to join Ralph and Jack in destructively
heaving a rock into the roof of the jungle in Chapter 1. But ironically, it
is through the least blameable and most saintly of the characters that
the revelation of mankind's diseased and fallen nature is made. Simon's
actions are portrayed as consistently unselfish: he cares for the littluns,
builds huts, tries to save Piggy from Jack's anger, crosses the island at
dusk to help Piggy and the littluns, encourages Ralph in his leadership,
and finally forces himself to climb the mountain to uncover the truth
about the Beast, only to be murdered by those whom he seeks to
liberate from fear by the truth he has painfully discovered. If any
character in the fable might be thought to be exempt from the 'essential
illness' of the human condition, it is Simon. He alone has the sheer
moral courage necessary to face and comprehend what it is that causes
the degeneration of the boys into squalor, savagery and bestiality. In
his confrontation with the spiked pig's head, he refuses to flinch from
the ultimate truth, which is that, like the Beast, and like everything outside ourselves that we call evil, it is in reality neutral, and is invested
with evil only because he himself projects on to it an evil that originates
in himself, but that is common to all mankind:

> You knew, didn't you? I'm part of you? Close, close, close!
> I'm the reason why it's no go? Why things are as they are?

Even if some critics consider Simon to be too contrived a mouthpiece
for Golding's central theme, they can hardly deny that in so far as the

fable can be claimed to have a 'message', this is the very heart of it. Ralph survives to know its truth and to weep 'for the end of innocence'.

4.2 CIVILISATION

The novel presents civilisation both positively and negatively. While the boys, with the exception of Piggy, are at first exhilarated at knowing that they are on their own, and therefore exempt from the imposition of the adult world and its standards, the littluns and the more responsible older boys quickly come to the realisation that being cut off from the authority of schoolmasters and parents carries severe penalties. Their very irresponsibility in starting a fire that destroys a littlun, or in gorging fruit that gives them diarrhoea, or in fouling their immediate surroundings, forces Ralph to take an adult role and insist on rules designed to achieve civilised standards and to maximise the possibility of rescue. Even so, the action of the story strips the boys bit by bit of the veneer of civilisation, which the boys abandon in much the same way as they abandon their school uniforms.

Ralph's rules are increasingly ignored and violated, then challenged and contemptuously dismissed by Jack. The authority of the conch shell, a symbol of rational discussion and civilised values, is slowly eroded; the shelters and signal fire are neglected. As their memories of civilisation fade, the majority of the boys revert to savagery, which liberates them from civilised rules and standards, but at the cost of their forfeiting their individuality to become members of a tribe dominated by a Chief who imposes his will with arbitrary brutality, stopping at neither torture nor murder.

Ralph, Piggy and Simon struggle to uphold civilised standards, but fail because these have literally to be worked at (building shelters, keeping clean), whereas Jack offers the alternative life of excitement and hunting, free of boring responsibilities. Still more importantly, Jack has an answer to the boys' fear of a Beast that increasingly menaces their lives. It can be killed, or at least placated. Ralph despairs at the way everything breaks up, and together with Piggy and Simon, prays for a sign from civilisation. We know from his daydreaming that civilisation for Ralph means the security and the comfort of a home; but it also means an ordered life, a respect for adult authority, decency and honesty in one's dealings with others, caring for the weak, and, as Piggy would say, it means a world that makes sense – 'with houses an' streets, an' – TV' – and therefore a world free from fear and the menace of a Beast.

The heavily ironic answer to Ralph, Piggy and Simon, who strive unsuccessfully 'to convey the majesty of adult life' and desperately plead for a sign, is the dead airman, who symbolises the dark and negative aspect of civilisation, and is mistakenly, but significantly, believed to be the Beast. An alert reader will have noted that throughout the story, there are implicit references to 'civilised' violence. From the first chapter on, the play and speech of the boys is infected with this: Ralph 'machine-guns' Piggy; the size of a rock is equated with a tank, and it plunges into the forest 'like a bomb'. The boys of *Lord of the Flies* are never innocent, as Ballantyne's much older boys are. What violates their innocence is the whole world they live in: a world of atomic war. Through it they come to the island, and when they are finally saved, it is by being taken aboard a warship. Piggy's faith in civilisation is shown to be ludicrously misplaced, since the scientific progress he so confidently affirms has left the world in ruins, just as Jack's savages leave their island world in ruins; and both are destroyed because boys and adults alike are at the mercy of their own bestiality. Piggy accuses the boys of acting 'like a crowd of kids', without seeing that adults behave *exactly* like kids, but on a dishearteningly grander scale, using atom bombs for sticks.

Piggy believes in reason and claims that 'life is scientific'. But it is precisely because of the narrowness of this belief, and the unrelatedness of scientific knowledge to a profounder understanding of our true selves, that disasters occur. 'Man's essential illness' comes from his failure to face up to his own 'diseased and fallen nature'. His pride in his own rationality, which is inseparable from his pride in civilisation, blinds him to the reality of himself, which he desperately fears, but dare not confront. This truth is thrust home in Chapter 10, where Piggy consistently denies the truth of what happened when Simon was murdered, even though Ralph has the moral courage to recall it with ambiguous 'loathing' and 'excitement'. 'We never done nothing, we never saw nothing,' Piggy stubbornly insists, and tries to explain away what cannot be explained away – the part he as a 'rational' human being played in the frenzy of the previous evening. Piggy, the most 'adult' of the boys, displays here what Golding calls 'the infinite cynicism of adult life'. It is a cynicism that in the adult world stops at nothing, not even nuclear war, which can be regarded as the definitive climax of civilisation. In some respects, Piggy's counterpart in the adult world is the naval officer, who represents the intrusion of the 'real' world into the fictional nightmare. The officer is, in fact, a 'cutout' figure, straight out of the innocent world of Ballantyne's *The Coral Island*. Overtly, he is civilised, just as overtly he is an adult; but his civilisation is no more than a well laundered uniform, and in understanding 'the darkness of man's heart' he is a mere child, compared with Ralph. Talk of the boys' being 'saved' is a nonsense, since the civilisation they hope to return to is 'in ruins', and as Golding himself has provocatively asked: 'Who will rescue the adult and the cruiser?' Civilisation, as presented in *Lord of the Flies*, is ambiguous and paradoxical.

4.3 FEAR AND THE BEAST

If *Lord of the Flies* presents man's diseased and fallen nature as his ultimate reality, it insistently shows that destructive, and self-destructive, violence is the inevitable outcome of this, and its release mechanism is fear. Setting aside the high-spirited horseplay of Chapter 1, virtually all the violence in the story has its origin in the tormenting fear extensively exposed in Chapter 2. Ralph calls an assembly to reassure the boys that they are on 'a good island', but almost immediately a littlun with a birth-mark shows distress, with talk about snake-things and a beastie that prowls the wood and wants to eat him. It is dusk. Shadows that are not just physical shadows close in on the assembly. The littluns need 'more than rational assurance' (a hint that there is something in their nature beyond the reach of reason), and all the boys shudder restlessly as the sun dies: a physical reaction indistinguishable from the fear that grips them. When the fire they then start goes out of control, the littlun with the birth-mark is destroyed by it, and the other littluns, their faces 'lit redly', scream like demons in hell as trees explode in flame round about them. The terror of this scene prefigures what lies ahead.

Chapter 5 offers an analysis of the boys' fears, which Ralph sees are the root cause of why 'things are breaking up'. He repeats his mistake of calling an assembly at dusk, when the encroaching shadows add an eeriness to the boys' already exaggerated terrors. Ralph confesses he himself feels fear, but insists there is no justification for it. Piggy denies its existence altogether, though he admits, with Jack in mind, that they all 'get frightened of people'. Jack, who when he hunts senses a menacing presence haunting him, denies that there is 'a dark thing, a beast, some sort of animal'; but his denials are less convincing than disturbing, and he ambiguously tells the littluns that they will have to put up with their fear, since as with 'the rest of us', that is their nature. Only Simon, 'inarticulate in his effort to express mankind's essential sickness', perceives the truth about fear, but he is shouted down. Talk about nightmares, giant squids, beasts from the sea, ghosts, only inflames the boys' imaginations, and Ralph realises too late that his attempt to dispel fear by open and rational discussion of it has badly backfired. His effort to discredit ghosts by means of a show of hands exposes the folly of supposing that terrors lodged in the deepest and darkest recesses of the boys' natures can be exorcised by opinion poll and democratic procedure.

Of the various attitudes portrayed towards fear, Piggy's is most intellectual, and *therefore* the shallowest and least comprehending. His pride in being 'scientific' not only prevents him from understanding the fear so distressingly obvious in the littluns, but also from understanding its origin in what Freud calls the 'unconscious mind' or 'Id', which is neither rational in itself, nor accessible to reason. He shows a glimpse of awareness when he acknowledges that being scared of someone can make you hate him, so that when you see him, 'it's like asthma and you can't breathe'; but it seems he does not really grasp that his asthma is his body's answer to other and deeper fears he 'scientifically' rejects.

While Ralph can at least admit to sharing some of the littluns' fears, it is Jack who is most fully aware of their sinister, instinctive nature. This enables him to play upon the fears of the others, sneering at them for giving way to a cowardice he has ruthlessly mastered in himself; and because he is alive to his own instinctive nature, he provides various solutions for coping with the Beast, which is an objectification of the boys' terrors. He and his hunters will track it down, hem it in, and kill it, ritually. The ritual is itself a means of bringing both the Beast and the boys' fears under control. Jack's primitive mentality also leads him to placate the Beast by offering it the pig's head. It is likely that the rituals in which the boys engage reflect the 'double-think' of unsophisticated minds. They know and do not know the truth about the Beast. They know and do not know that it is both inside themselves and external to them. They know and do not know that it cannot be killed.

Neither intellectual arrogance nor submission to blind instinct keeps Simon from confronting the truth, however unpleasant it might be. He is determined to understand things comprehensively and has the moral nerve to face the consequences. Even when he feels the onset of an epileptic fit, and stands before the impaled pig's head, he resists the hallucinatory voice that offers him the easy way out. The Lord of the Flies attempts to bully him into believing he is no more than 'an ignorant, silly little boy', who had better rejoin the others, before they think he is more 'batty' than ever. Though he shakes with fear, he stands his ground when the pig's head declares it is the Beast, 'the reason why it's no go', and threatens him prophetically with 'being done' by the boys. Nothing the Beast says is new to Simon, who speaks aloud in answer to it: 'I know that'. He also knows that its voice originates in him, as does the fear it appears to generate and the evil it counsels him to accept. It invites him to identify with Jack and his hunters who create the Beast out of their own fear and then mistake it for reality. Simon 'licks his dry lips', feels the weight of his own hair, senses the savagery inside himself and finally falls in an epileptic fit. He arrives at 'that ancient, inescapable recognition' of his own bestiality, and has the moral strength to accept the darkest truths about his own nature. But this acceptance strips the pig's head of its terror and its claim to be the Beast. The terror and the Beast are 'close, close, close', because they are ineradicably a part of himself, just as the blackness that spreads about him when he falls in a fit originates, not in the objective world about him, but in what is happening inside himself.

Simon loses his life by attempting to reveal this truth to others, who suffer torments of terror for a Beast they locate in the sea or jungle or mountain top – anywhere but where it really exists: in themselves, and above all in their collectivity. Trying to free them from fear of the Beast, Simon is himself identified with it, and accordingly destroyed. When he dies, the truth of his discovery dies with him. Ralph dare not and cannot see the pig's head for what it is: he lashes out at it in 'sick fear' and loathing, only to be mocked by its leering grin 'now six feet across'. The obscenity lords itself over him, and as he is hunted down, he becomes indistinguishable from the savages who pursue him: he is 'screaming, snarling, bloody'; the personification of terror – 'fear on flying feet'.

4.4 POWER

The narrative of *Lord of the Flies* recounts the unequal struggle for power that takes place between Ralph, who is the elected leader of the boys, and Jack, who usurps his leadership. Ralph is tolerant by nature, willing to take the advice of others, especially Piggy, and careful to follow the democratic procedures symbolised in the conch shell. However, his virtues serve only to undermine his authority and bring about his downfall.

Jack, on the other hand, is eaten up by ambition; he has the mentality of a Fascist, and a total disregard for those who are weaker than himself. From the start, he dominates his choirboys like a regimental sergeant major, and shows not the least concern when Simon faints. He succeeds in 'liberating' himself and his hunters into savagery and he is obsessed with killing, which is the ultimate assertion of power. After he and his hunters kill their first pig, Jack is elated with 'the knowledge that they had outwitted a living thing, imposed their will upon it, taken away its life like a long satisfying drink'. The 'thick excitement' Jack feels in killing a pig leads on to the murder of Simon, then Piggy, and to the near-murder of Ralph, whom he *must* destroy, not simply because Ralph has been his rival, but paradoxically because he has a sneaking liking for him. But, for the sake of power, Jack is prepared to be as ruthless with himself as with others. He is under a compulsion to obliterate all opposition to himself and to destroy whatever he is unable to control. He even eliminates his individual identity to set himself up as a tribal Chief, with life and death at his command, and finally he sits 'like an idol' on his throne, exhibiting power 'in the brown swell of his forearms'. Authority is said to sit on his shoulders, where it 'chatters in his ear like an ape': an image that fittingly conveys the brutal and brutish nature of the power he wields.

The one occasion on which Jack actually seems childish is when his challenge to Ralph's leadership apparently fails in Chapter 8, and he weeps with humiliation. He accuses Ralph of not being a prefect, and in language that echoes a British playground, declares he is 'not going to play any longer'. Suddenly we cease to see Jack as a threatening savage, and are aware that he is still a child. At the same time, we are alerted to the childishness of the power game that so obsessively preoccupies him.

In Chapter 3 we are given an insight into the fascination that a sense of power has for a littlun called Henry. He pokes about on the shore with a stick, making runnels to trap the tiny scavenging organisms brought in by the tide, and becomes 'absorbed beyond mere happiness' as he feels himself 'exercising control over living things'. Squatting at the water's edge, he is rapt in 'the illusion of mastery'. Meanwhile, Roger watches him, then teases him by throwing stones close to him, but aimed to miss, because 'round the squatting child' is 'the protection of parents and school and policemen and the law' – the authority of a civilisation that as yet still 'conditions' his arm. But just as Henry is absorbed in playfully exercising power over the 'transparencies', so Roger in his turn playfully dominates Henry, and even blushes at being caught out, because deep within himself he senses a satisfaction that is touched by something deeper than mere play.

In fact, Roger graduates from teasing to torture, and offers the clearest example of the perversion of power which we call sadism. This is shown in the killing of the sow (Chapter 8) where Roger cruelly lodges his spear in the sow's anus and forces it forward with all his weight till 'the terrified squealing' becomes 'a high pitched scream'. There is a clear hint of sadism, too, in Jack's arbitrary beating of Wilfred (Chapter 10), and it is this incident that comes to Roger like 'an illumination', opening up a whole new world to him: 'He...sat still, assimilating the possibilities of irresponsible authority.' From this point on, Roger seeks the fulfilment of his perverted nature in the infliction of pain and death. His arm is no longer conditioned by memories of civilisation. When Roger, Piggy and the twins make their way into Castle Rock (Chapter 11), he aims a stone to miss the twins, and when Sam dangerously stumbles, 'some source of power' begins 'to pulse in Roger's body'. Minutes later, he leans his weight on the lever that topples the rock that kills Piggy, 'with a sense of delirious abandonment', and in his haste to torture the captured twins he 'only just' avoids pushing Jack with his shoulder. In Roger, who finds pleasure in the physical pain he inflicts, we witness the excesses of a power that has become so corrupt that it sets him apart, even among Jack's savages. 'A hangman's horror' clings round him, and he wields an authority that is 'nameless, unmentionable'.

4.5 REALITY AND ILLUSION

Throughout the novel, there is a preoccupation with what is real and what is illusory. Even the island is ambiguously presented: 'the filmy enchantment of mirage' and 'strange glamour' on the lagoon side give it an unreal quality, while 'the brute obtuseness of the ocean' on its exposed side numbs the mind with a sense of a reality indifferent, and alien to, all human hopes and purposes. The effects of light and darkness affect the boys' perceptions. Places and objects that are ordinary by daylight become horrifying in the dark. In the 'tangle of golden reflections' Ralph speculates in a way that is foreign to him on the faces of the assembly, asking himself: 'If faces were different when lit from above or below – what was a face? What was anything?' (Chapter 5). Meanwhile, Jack has successfully set an example to his savages by abandoning civilised standards for a painted mask that makes him seem 'an awesome stranger', even to himself. But it is through the illusion of their masks that the boys are enabled to realise their true natures, while paradoxically forfeiting their personal identities.

There are many other similarly disconcerting ironies. The 'fun and games' the boys look forward to turn from play into frightening ritual and finally into murder. What Ralph and Piggy and Simon think of with awe as 'the majesty of adult life' is a pure delusion, since the savagery of the boys is being perpetrated by adults on the appropriately larger scale of atomic warfare. Their hopes focus on rescue and on being 'saved'; but the civilisation they believe they will be returned to no longer exists. The Beast itself is taken for reality by apparently healthy, normal boys, though it is in fact illusory. Meanwhile the illusion (and the central truth of the novel) is understood by a shy, inarticulate oddity of a little boy, who faints, has fits and distractedly walks into a tree. Simon, who alone knows no objective Beast exists, is murdered by boys who deludedly believe that *he* is the Beast. At the story's close the real world apparently reasserts itself in the person of the naval officer, but he is only outwardly 'adult', and the little boys who stand before him shaking and sobbing know a reality he is too naïve even to suspect.

The shift in perspective brought about by the arrival of the naval office is only the most notable of many such shifts designed by the author in his handling of the theme of reality and illusion. By his references to the remote and alien ocean heaving like some 'stupendous beast', or to the tides that 'soon, in a matter of centuries' will make an island of Castle Rock, or to the 'steadfast constellations' shining down on Simon's dead body, Golding startlingly alters the human scale of space and time, so distancing action and characters alike by setting them under the eye of eternity.

5 TECHNICAL FEATURES

5.1 PLOT AND STRUCTURE

As a narrative, *Lord of the Flies* is fast-moving and without either sub-
plot or unnecessary digressions. Its themes are clearly stated in the first
half, with more than a hint of foreboding and menace, then ironically
reworked at a deeper, more anguished and frightening level in the
second half.

The novel's development is *revelatory* – that is to say, it begins by
revealing first a little, then more, then a great deal, about the characters
and their behaviour. Repetition, with some variation, enriches the
reader's insight into what, at the deepest level, the novel is about. Far
from being monotonous, it is the means of heightening tension, and this
is because each repetition adds something new and more powerfully
charged to what has gone before: it is *incremental* repetition. The initial,
innocent excitement of exploring the island (Chapter 1), is satirised in
the second exploration (Chapter 7), in which the boys search out the
Beast. Roger begins to realise his true nature by aiming stones that just
miss a littlun, and finishes by toppling the rock that destroys Piggy.
Between Jack's initial attempt to kill a piglet, when the 'enormity' of
what he tries to do leads to failure, and the sharpening of the stick at
both ends when Ralph is hunted down, there are several stages, each
more sickening than the one before. Meanwhile, the ritual chanting
switches from 'Kill the pig!' to 'Kill the beast!', and what begins as a
game turns into deadly and murderous reality, with Simon a sacrificial
victim. The fire in Chapter 2, which has the boys mischievously 'shrieking with laughter', also claims a victim and reveals a first glimpse of
'hell'. In the last chapter, the island is ablaze like the whole of hell,
while the boys themselves act as destructively and maliciously as devils.

The pace increases and the tension builds up throughout, as with the best of adventure stories; but the structure of the novel, through repetition, accumulative progression, and climax, relates to much more than the narrative. Even unsophisticated readers can sense some deeper significance underlying and underpinning the story's surface. References such as those to 'mankind's essential sickness' and 'the loss of innocence' can hardly fail to alert the reader to this, and once we begin to penetrate the narrative events and characters, we quickly perceive that they afford rich insights into the human condition. The novel has unignorable elements of allegory and fable, and the point about allegory and fable is that they are to a great extent *consciously* controlled by the author. Before he set pen to paper, Golding had already conceived the novel's major theme and its outcome: he wished to challenge the facile optimism of Ballantyne's *The Coral Island* by writing about 'real boys on an island, showing what a mess they'd make'. This is precisely what he does, but as he himself was aware, his island, his boys and the mess they make, are richly invested with symbolic meaning. As Golding has written:

> The theme is an attempt to trace the defects of society back to the defects of human nature. . .The whole book is symbolic in nature, except the rescue in the end where adult life appears, dignified and capable, but in reality enmeshed in the same evil as the symbolic life of the children on the island.

We should not, therefore, that the symbolic needs of the novel necessarily affect structure and significantly determine both the action and the characters. It is a tribute to Golding's supreme literary skill, that the story and the symbolic significance cohere so perfectly that we respond to them both simultaneously. Often when we read allegory and fable, we are painfully conscious that the characters and events stand for something *other than themselves*: they fail to operate convincingly at different levels. But in *Lord of the Flies*, the realism *embodies* the other levels of meaning; and it does so subtly, suggesting a range of symbolic meaning that cannot be crudely reduced to a one to one correspondence. Jack is, of course, a savage, a murderer and a Nazi, just as Ralph is a democrat and Piggy is an intellectual; but they are all more subtly conceived than this suggests, and are too complex to be labelled and written off in this naïve way. So it is with the setting and action. The island is vividly realised, though it is a microcosm; the boys are convincingly individualised, however much their characters imply political attitudes; and the rise of Jack at Ralph's expense is painfully true to life, however much the stages of his success mark the cumulative triumph of bad over good.

There are, however, a very few events in the story that relate to structure and have been found too contrived by some critics, most notably the 'sign' sent from the adult world (Chapter 6), in the form of the dead airman. This may appear too cynical and too pat an answer to Ralph and his friends, who naïvely believe in 'the majesty of adult life'. Similarly, it has been objected that the wind's lifting the corpse to a sea-burial at just the time that the tide claims Simon's body (Chapter 9) is too artificial – that is to say, the symbolism fails to cohere with a credible naturalism. There is room for varying opinions about the acceptability of the dead airman and his role in the story, but objections raised about the naval officer's sudden intrusion into the climax of Chapter 12 are usually misconceived. Of course this intrusion is unforeseen and wholly incredible in its timing; but as Golding says, there is nothing symbolic about it. On the contrary, it comes as an antidote to the story's symbolism and is a deliberate device to shock the reader with a reality that throws everything that has happened into a new and startling perspective (a device, incidentally, Golding uses in *Pincher Martin* and elsewhere).

5.2 CHARACTERISATION

Whatever deeper meanings *Lord of the Flies* may have, we should never forget that it is overtly an adventure story. That it is a *successful* adventure story depends in large measure on its portraying recognisable characters with whom we can sympathise and identify. First and foremost, Golding has to win our acceptance of his boys *as boys*. Having achieved this, he is then able to invest individual characters with traits and qualities that transcend the individual and afford us insights into different human types, or at the deepest level of all, into the human condition itself. Indeed, it is Golding's distinction to have created characters who are wholly credible at a realistic level, while they remain powerfully persuasive both as types and at a symbolic level.

When we are first introduced to the characters, they are not only boys, in a naturalistic sense, but boys who are more themselves than ever because they are liberated from adult control. Ralph stands on his hands in pure joy, and in the same spirit joins Jack and Simon in heaving a great rock into the canopy of the forest to schoolboy exclamations of 'Wacco', 'Whee-aa-oo!' and 'Golly!' In fact, the datedness of the slang pinpoints them not simply as schoolboys, but as schoolboys of the immediate post-Second World War period. Like boys anywhere, they respond excitedly to what they see as an adventure (an adult would call their being wrecked, with loss of life, a disaster), and their understanding of their condition relates to school stories. They are too young to grasp the horrors that have overtaken the world from which they have been evacuated, and throughout they entertain an illogical belief in its being still as they remember it. Even Piggy continues to believe in a civilisation – 'houses an' streets, an' – TV' – that lies in ruins, and Simon reassures Ralph that he will get back to it, when clearly there is nothing to get back to.

The small boys are never really individualised, but there is much more differentiation among the older boys. Their physical differences are noted, and their differences of temperament become apparent the moment they talk with one another and begin to form relationships. The boyish boasting between Ralph and Piggy in their first encounter reveals much more than the difference in their social backgrounds. Ralph is obviously conscious of being in every way Piggy's superior and soon drops a cool politeness for casual abuse of this fat boy whose only claim to fame is that he gets 'ever so many sweets'. But we recognise, too, that Piggy is intellectually more mature than Ralph in their exchange about the possibility of rescue. Then again, we at once see how very different Jack is from either Ralph or Piggy, the moment he marches his choir along the beach, shouting orders with 'offhand authority', and announcing that he is Merridew – not just a 'kid', with a kid's name – and ought to be chief. And what could be more individual, even idiosyncratic, than the way in which Simon shyly strokes Ralph's arm, to show his affection? As the story develops, so our understanding of the individuality of the older boys, including that of Sam and Eric, who constitute a single identity, also develops, and our sense of the characters' individuality is heightened by the tensions that arise among them.

However, in so far as they revert to primitive behaviour, they lose individuality. This is obvious in respect of Jack, who forfeits his identity to wear a mask, and finally becomes an anonymous tribal chief; but it is true of *all* the boys when they frenziedly act as 'a single organism' in killing Simon.

It is not difficult to recognise that, though individually conceived, several of the bigger boys exemplify *types* of character. Conspicuously, Ralph and Jack typify, on the one hand, an easy-going, tolerant, democratic, and civilised way of life, and on the other hand, a way of life that is rigid, ruthless, Fascist and savage. Piggy has the strengths and weaknesses of the intellectual, Simon has the compassionate insight of a saint, Roger embodies our worst sadistic impulses and Sam and Eric typify ordinary humanity, who are basically decent, but too easily exploited and dominated by ruthless leadership. Their representative function does not, however, impair their claim to be individual characters. It is sometimes said that Simon is not a boy, but a vehicle to express the spiritual awareness of the author. But he wrestles jubilantly with Ralph, as any boy would, and shares the exhilaration all the boys feel in finding they have an island to themselves. Similarly, Piggy has been argued to be no more than an intellectual Billy Bunter, though in fact he achieves a kind of nobility, both when he harangues the boys for starting the fire that destroys the 'littlun' with the birthmark, and when he carries the conch on his fatal visit to Castle Rock.

Closely allied to what the characters typify, but at a still more elemental level, is what they symbolise in terms of the story. For example, when we see Piggy, nearly blind, groping his way to Castle Rock in a desperate, last attempt to reason with Jack, we are aware that rationality and savagery, the enlightened and the dark forces of our humanity are closing in a final conflict. The fragile conch Piggy carries, which is invested with civilised values, smashes to smithereens at the same time as Piggy's skull spills out the brains by which mankind evolved civilisation. Simon's death, too, is not simply the death of a rather strange boy, but symbolises the end of intuitive understanding and goodness. The message Simon sacrifices his life to deliver – the truth that he alone had the moral courage to uncover – goes unheard, drowned by the frenzy of the ritual death-chant.

It is customary to think of characters as 'developing' or 'revealed'. A developed character is one who in the course of the novel is significantly changed by the action, while a revealed character remains static, though we learn more about him as the action unfolds. Ralph is the only real instance of the first (he finishes a much sadder and wiser boy than he began); the others, like Jack, are 'liberated' into savagery, but reveal nothing new in their nature. The 'illumination' that Roger has does not alter him; on the contrary, it leaves him free to fulfil his essential nature by murder and torture. And this descent into savagery itself destroys character. In so far as the boys revert to primitive behaviour, they lose whatever individuality they originally possessed. Jack has to forfeit his identity to wear a mask, and finally becomes a wholly anonymous tribal chief. When frenzy takes hold of *all* the boys in their killing of Simon, individuality ceases to exist: they act in the grip of a primitive compulsion that nullifies character and reduces the whole lot of them to the mindlessness of a mob – 'a single organism'.

Ralph

Twelve years old, well-built, fair-haired and middle-class, Ralph has some of the obvious characteristics of a schoolboy hero and leader. He is, as the other boys are quick to recognise, well balanced, decent and very *normal*, unlike Piggy, the intellectual, Jack, the fanatic, and Simon, solitary and strange. His dependability and normality stem from his secure home background, which means a great deal to him, and of which he dreams and daydreams more and more as 'things break up' in the island adventure that goes wrong. It is part of Ralph's normality that he has only average intelligence. His leadership is buttressed from the start by the more intelligent Piggy. For example, the conch shell is no more than 'a worthy plaything' to Ralph. Its use as a horn to summon the stranded boys, and the authority it is increasingly invested with, are first perceived by Piggy, who often unobtrusively manipulates Ralph, the overt leader. When despairing or perplexed, Ralph is not above openly asking Piggy for advice.

But whatever his intelligence, Ralph is almost always fair-minded. He takes his leadership seriously, with some occasional prompting from Piggy, and sets about making proper provision for everyone, and especially the littluns, who most need it. When the other boys shirk their duties, to play or swim or hunt, Ralph tries with steady determination to build shelters. When he is voted chief, he is sensitive to Jack's disappointment, and tries to avoid conflict by consigning the choir to Jack as hunters, so showing a restraint and fair-mindedness Jack himself would have been utterly incapable of. Right to the story's end, he is tempted to believe that the other boys must share his own basic decency and sense of justice.

> ...might it not be possible to walk boldly into the fort, say – "I've got pax", laugh lightly and sleep among the others?

However, horrors of darkness and death prevail, and Ralph has to face the tragic reality that Golding calls 'the darkness of man's heart'. Though he is tempted to think of Simon's and Piggy's deaths as 'an accident', he cannot in the end do so, because he remains honest with himself. After Simon's death, Piggy evades facing facts, pretending everything that happened was accidental; but Ralph is morally Piggy's superior, not only because he can openly acknowledge his own part in Simon's death, but because in doing so he glimpses something of Simon's vision ('I'm frightened. Of us.'), and can even recall the murder with 'loathing, and at the same time a kind of feverish excitement'.

Golding speaks of Ralph's mild eyes, which proclaim him 'no devil'. But he is by no means a saint, either. He can share the hunters' excitement and bloodlust, and he boasts immoderately about spearing the boar's snout. Equally, he can share the other boys' irresponsible delight in play and having fun; he can even share their rather cruel laughter at Piggy's expense. His courage is certainly equal to Jack's, as he proves by deciding to climb the mountain to discover the Beast, and by forcing himself to take the lead and make the 'two leaden steps' that finally reveal it. A strong sense of duty can make him courageous, but his fear can on occasion overwhelm his physical courage, and even his moral courage. When Jack brings his hunters to the shelter in the night to steal Piggy's glasses, Ralph mistakes the noises they make for the approach of the Beast. The blood roars in his head, and very *un*heroically he prays that the Beast will 'prefer littluns'.

Ralph is all the more credible for such inconsistencies of character, and we should remember that he is tested in extreme and violent ways. His tendency to be easy-going and liberal, allied to his good nature, is exploited by Jack, who is ruthlessly single-minded, and quite without the self-doubt that at times undermines Ralph's leadership. Piggy has to alert Ralph to the threat and hatred posed by Jack, and Ralph is so far from having a dark side to his nature that even on the eve of his planned execution he can talk about his having liked Jack. Meanwhile, he is slow to grasp the significance of the stick sharpened at both ends, and 'Samneric' have actually to warn him about Roger's sadism.

As Ralph himself comes to realise, he is inadequate as a thinker, and his judgements often suffer in consequence. Only very gradually does he come to respect Piggy's capacity to think. His limited understanding keeps him from taking Jack's measure, so that Jack can taunt him into acting against his own better judgement, as when they climb the mountain together to the Beast. Some of Ralph's decisions are extremely ill-judged. His calling an assembly as dusk settles on the island is a mistake that gets disastrously out of hand when, in Chapter 2, the talk focuses on snake-things and beasties; and Ralph's attempt to deal with the littluns' fears by holding a democratic vote on whether beasties exist is both pathetic and ludicrous.

But we must allow for the unremitting and unfair strain Ralph is subjected to. He is, after all, only twelve years old, but he has to try to think and act like a responsible adult, and it is no wonder that he fails. The tension and strain he is under are more than enough to set him biting his nails (or, finally, biting the bark off his spear), and it is small wonder that his mind keeps blacking out when, despite his courageous efforts to get the boys to concentrate on rescue and to work together co-operatively, they choose 'liberation' into savagery, while the world of sane values and moral obligation he represents falls chaotically apart. Just how much civilisation means to him is clear from the almost hysterical disappointment he feels when in Chapter 4 the chance of rescue is lost, and the 'understandable and lawful world' seems to slip away with the ship.

Jack

From the start, Jack asserts his claims to leadership, and is unrelenting in struggling to achieve it. If he could yield to anyone, it would be to

Ralph, for whom he feels, initially at least, a certain respect and shy liking, if only because at first Ralph shares his adventurous delight in being free from the restraints of the adult world. His limited tolerance of Ralph is encouraged by Ralph's helping him to heave a great rock into the canopy of the forest, in the course of exploring the island, and by Ralph's unsympathetic treatment of Piggy. Gradually, as Ralph becomes more responsible in his behaviour, and treats Piggy with increasing respect, Jack becomes more and more alienated from Ralph, and more and more violent in his bullying of Piggy, whom he intensely resents for being physically handicapped and an intellectual. He uses Piggy to taunt Ralph with, and is obviously jealous. 'We mustn't let anything happen to Piggy, must we?' he sneers, speaking 'in a queer, tight voice' (Chapter 7).

A tall, thin, ugly, red-headed boy, Jack first makes his appearance at the head of the choir, over whom he exercises a strict military control. The choir vote for him to be leader, but do so out of fear, not liking. He wears to the end a black cap that carries appropriate overtones of his being an executioner, and throughout the story shadows, 'the damp darkness of the forest' and the threat of death cling about him. There is no hint of kindness or sympathy in him. His opaque eyes – eyes bolting and blinded by fanaticism – disregard Simon when he faints, and are indifferent to the needs of the littluns, whose fears he is willing to exploit for his own ends. He is obsessed by his passion for power, at whatever cost, and gradually realises his own nature by exercising this power in its most extreme form, determining the life and death not only of animals, but of his rivals. The justification of power does not concern him. In the end, he forfeits his own individuality to become a savage Chief, with total and arbitrary authority. Even his name is abandoned, along with all other tokens and memories of the civilised world. He beats Wilfred to satisfy a whim, demands absolute obedience and ritualised obeisance from his tribe, and caring nothing whatever for justice, compulsively seeks to destroy its last representative, Ralph.

Even so, Jack has to overcome in himself certain civilised restraints which he regards as weaknesses. He cannot at first commit the enormity of killing a pig, but slamming his knife into a tree trunk, vows he will not let a second chance slip. Nor does he; but his triumph in making a kill and providing meat is ruined by Ralph's accusation that it has been achieved at the cost of their missing the chance of being saved. This infuriates Jack, since his need to hunt and kill is more immediate and urgent than his need to be rescued. Even so, he has to hide behind a mask of paint and he twitches still, as he boasts of cutting the pig's throat. Only later will he kill, and lug out the guts, and break all previous taboos, as with grim determination he gradually suppresses all civilised emotions in himself as shameful. Meanwhile, imposing his will, outwitting a living creature and taking its life are, for Jack, 'like a long satisfying drink'. His anger at not winning Ralph's applause for his first kill (an anger he takes out on Piggy because he dare not at this stage risk direct conflict with Ralph) shows him to be to an extent vulnerable. 'I painted my face - I stole up. Now you eat - all of you...' he says in rage and frustration, precisely because he has had to nerve himself to kill. He still, at this stage, wants sympathetic 'understanding' of what he has had to put himself through to achieve success, but all he gets from the boys is 'respect'. This serves only to harden his nature still more.

But Jack is no less severe with himself in coping with fears and superstition. He accepts fear as a reality that cannot be avoided, and expects everyone else, including the littluns, to do so; he understands the littluns' fears better than the other biguns just because of his super-stitious sense of being the *quarry*, not the hunter, when he stalks the forest. The atavistic impulse is strong in Jack: at the beginning of Chapter 3 he is described in images that are primitive, elemental, and even animal – he seems less a hunter, 'than a furtive thing, ape-like among the tangle of trees'. But this same impulse helps him to find a primitive solution to the problem of his own and the boys' tormented fears. He discovers how painted nakedness can liberate the personality 'from shame and self-consciousness'; he initiates dancing after killing the pig, sensing that ritual serves to release and at the same time control powerful emotions; he similarly placates the Beast by leaving it the offering of a pig's head.

It would be wrong, however, to suppose that Jack cannot think, when it suits his purpose. He is first to realise that Piggy's spectacles (which he later claims as a trophy) can be put to use as burning glasses, and when he takes the conch he speaks with cleverness and cunning, playing on the boys' fears, but also making debating points against Ralph. In Chapter 8, he actually calls an assembly to challenge Ralph's leadership, and is hard-hitting in arguing that Ralph is a talker, like Piggy, who fails to value the hunters and is (though this is a lie) a coward. He fails in this challenge to be leader, and goes off on his own, weeping 'humiliating tears'; but his failure is apparent, rather than real, since most of the boys desert Ralph to join Jack's tribe, so making him 'brilliantly happy'. After this, however, Jack submerges his identity in his role of chief. He becomes remote, 'like an idol', surrounded by more ritual of his own devising, and rules tyrannically over his tribe. The authority he so passionately pursued now sits 'on his shoulders and chatters in his ear like an ape'.

In Chapter 2 Jack gives apparent backing to Ralph in calling for rules, with penalties for those who break them:

> ...'We've got to have rules and obey them. After all, we're not savages. We're English; and the English are best at everything...'

This patriotic sentiment is identical with Ballantyne's. But it is subjected to the author's darkest and most persistent irony. Jack is the first to ignore democratic rules and to plunge into savagery. This does not mean he is against rules. On the contrary, he is entirely *for* rules, once it is understood that his word is law. Rules, and harsh punishment for those who break them, are an absolute necessity for an intensely Fascist mentality like Jack's.

Piggy

We know Piggy only by his nickname, and Golding, like most of the boys, enjoys a joke at his expense, since he often uses a vocabulary associated with pigs ('grunt', 'squeak', etc.) in referring to him. Several things conspire to make him an outsider: his asthma, his fatness and laziness, his tendency to fuss, his comparative intellectual maturity, his poor eyesight, his being fatherless and brought up by an aunt, and his being working-class in speech and background. It is clear from the first that Piggy himself recognises that he is an outsider. He does all he can to ingratiate himself with Ralph, whose athletic body he watches enviously, though Ralph's initial reactions are to patronise him, to abuse him in a casual way because of his 'ass-mar' and aunt, and to betray his nickname, which was given by Piggy in confidence. Piggy's shortcomings are immediately obvious and invite ridicule; his merits require time and experience to be appreciated.

Despite his being the most bookish and intellectual of the boys, he can be childish on occasion. Ralph establishes his status by boasting that his father is a commander in the Navy. Piggy, who is perhaps illegitimate, makes his claim to fame in terms of his auntie's sweet shop, and his getting 'ever so many sweets'. His greed is, of course, a childish feature. In Chapter 1, though fearful of being separated from Ralph, he steals away to gorge fruit; in Chapter 4 he dribbles and pleads humiliatingly for meat; and in Chapter 9 he rationalises his greed by suggesting that he and Ralph should attend Jack's feast, 'to make sure nothing happens'. In fact, Simon is murdered.

Because he is physically weak, unfit and short-sighted, Piggy is timid and easily frightened. The moment he sees Jack, he knows that he will be bullied by him, and he clings loyally to Ralph because his instinct tells him that if Ralph were to 'stand out of the way' Jack would 'hurt the next thing', which is himself. For all his pretentions to be grown-up and scientific, he shares many of the fears felt by the others, including horror of the Beast reported by 'Samneric'. Jack sneers at Ralph for keeping Piggy 'out of danger', and certainly there is nothing heroic in his character; but this does not mean that he is a coward, or that he cannot be moved to act bravely on occasion, especially when his righteous indignation is aroused. Piggy achieves an incongruous dignity when in Chapter 2 he launches into a tirade, reproaching the others for behaving 'like a pack of kids', for not giving Ralph time to think, and for stupidly starting a fire that destroys the littlun with the mark on his face. When outraged, he can defy Jack, and he meets his death as a result of his insisting on doing so, despite Ralph's warning that he will get hurt. His last words are typical of him, and bravely spoken: 'Which is better – to have rules and agree, or to hunt and kill?'

Illness has kept Piggy isolated, given him time to reflect, and to acquire a more adult way of thinking than the others, whom he castigates for acting 'like kids'. Though he does not always live up to 'the majesty of adult life', as he conceives it, he believes fervently in it. Life is, for him, 'scientific': the world is rationally planned, with 'houses an' streets, an' – TV', all of which are strictly incompatible with ghosts and superstition. His profoundly serious respect for adult values makes him unimaginative and often the butt of the other boys' humour. Though Ralph is his intellectual inferior, he can pull Piggy's leg very easily; for example, about making a sundial or a steam engine. Meanwhile, and ironically, the world of scientific progress that Piggy confidently affirms is a world 'in ruins'.

Piggy is right to stick loyally by Ralph, whose basic decency can be relied on, and he realises that his own more 'grown-up' values stand no chance of being implemented, except through Ralph's agency. From the start, he tries persistently to influence and manipulate Ralph. He sees the possibility that the conch shell may be more than 'a plaything', and it is largely through his perception that it evolves into a symbol for democratic procedure, rules and law and order. For this reason, he passionately reveres the conch, bravely tries to protect it when Jack and his savages make a night attack, and proudly carries it to Castle Rock, to show Jack 'the one thing he hasn't got'. What he fails to see is that Jack does not want it, anyhow, and that it is – like the values it represents – exceedingly fragile. It is absolutely fitting that the shell should meet its end along with Piggy, exploding on the same rock that breaks open his skull.

Ralph is right when he acknowledges Piggy's superior intellect and laments 'the fall through the air of the true, wise friend called Piggy'. Even so, we are made aware of Piggy's limitations – for lack of a better word, his *spiritual* limitations – in his dealings with and attitude towards Simon. When Ralph has intuition enough to guess that Simon has gone off to climb the mountain, Piggy breaks into 'noisy laughter' and declares Simon 'cracked'. His intellect is unable to grasp the essential goodness and bravery of Simon, who turns to him for 'help and sympathy' in the assembly in Chapter 8, only to find on Piggy's face 'an expression of derisive incomprehension'. Worse still is Piggy's attempt to explain away Simon's death. He suggests every possible way out of facing the truth, but as even Ralph knows, all Piggy's arguments are specious and spurious. This attempt by Piggy to evade all moral guilt exposes how totally inadequate and even dishonest the intellect is when confronted with values that transcend its own limitations.

We should note that the progressive harms inflicted on Piggy – his becoming half blind, then almost entirely blind – correspond to the stages of the boys' retreat from civilised standards into an irrational savagery.

Simon

Golding himself has said of Simon that he is 'a saint', 'a Christ-figure', 'a lover of mankind, a visionary'. He is rather younger than the biguns, bright-eyed, 'a skinny, vivid little boy', with coarse black hair. His physical weakness is apparent from his fainting, and he probably is an epileptic. Unlike Piggy, who exploits his lack of fitness and uses it as an excuse for laziness, Simon is passionately determined to triumph over his body's frailty, whether he struggles to make shelters with Ralph, or stoically forces himself to climb the mountain. In sheer will-power, he outstrips all the other boys, even Jack; and unlike Jack, he directs it always towards ends that are constructive and good.

Simon's 'saintly' disposition is indicated in many ways. He genuinely cares for the littluns, reaches down fruit for them, builds huts for their security, and volunteers to cross the island at dusk on his own, to bring reassurance to them and Piggy. When Jack attacks Piggy for not helping with the fire, Simon quietly points out that because they used Piggy's spectacles, 'he helped that way'. Later, Simon self-sacrificingly shoves meat over the rocks to Piggy, from whom Jack is cruelly withholding it. Finally, Simon meets a kind of martyr's death, trying to bring to his murderers the reassurance of the truth he has discovered about the Beast.

No one understands Simon. Jack despises him as a weakling. Piggy fails to accord him even gratitude, and sees him as merely 'cracked'. Ralph respects Simon's merits ('He helps.'), and has just enough sensitiveness to guess what Simon may be doing when he goes missing; but he cannot fathom Simon's strangeness, which he thinks 'queer' and 'funny'. Certainly there are occasions when Simon's behaviour seems odd: he shows his liking for Ralph by shyly stroking his arm, and walks into a tree in what seems to be a trance. The fact is, Simon is sensitive to a whole range of experience from which the others are cut off. His understanding is strongly intuitive, but his excessive shyness, especially when he tries to speak in the assemblies, combines with the difficulty he has in articulating his intuition to render him fumbling and inarticulate, an object of scorn and ridicule. He is never given a fair hearing. Jack makes a dirty joke out of what he says; Piggy responds to his suggestion that the Beast may be only themselves by shouting 'Nuts!'.

Simon's intuition is such that it answers the intuition in the other boys. When Jack gropes for words to express what it is the littluns fear, Simon is quick to complete Jack's train of thought, suggesting that perhaps it is not 'a good island'. The other boys sense the growing antagonism between Ralph and Jack, but before they do, Simon seems to look into the future, and what he sees makes him afraid. Similarly, he is sensitive to Ralph's darkest fears, urging him to 'go on being chief', when he despairs. At the same time, Simon speaks with prophetic insight, assuring Ralph that he will 'get back all right' - an assurance that Ralph clings to desperately when, after Simon's death, he is hunted down like an animal.

But Simon is never more fully himself than when he is alone, which is something none of the others voluntarily choose to be. He is apparently unafraid of the forest, in which he makes a secret 'cabin' for himself, where he can respond undisturbed to the sights, colours, smells and sounds of the island, which he knows receptively, in all its organic complexity. Unlike the other boys, who ignore nature, except in so far as it serves their selfish purposes, Simon feels the unity of nature's life, and can surrender his own identity to it.

Perhaps as a result of such experience, Simon cannot share the other boys' superstitious dread of a Beast. As he tells Ralph, who is nerving himself to climb the mountain, he does not believe in a Beast. However he thinks of it, there rises 'before his inward sight the picture of a human at once heroic and sick'. But this intuition is backed up with tremendous moral courage. Though he is jeered at for saying so, he realises the necessity to face and reveal what it is that is on the mountain top. In the end, he knows that if this is to be done, he himself will have to do it, for, as he says, 'What else is there to do?'

Simon is committed to *understanding* (not simply to knowing, as Piggy may sometimes be said to know). But just how much courage it takes fully to understand something is clear from Simon's encounter with the Lord of the Flies. He has witnessed the bestiality of the killing, and confronted by the pig's head, he is subjected to an hallucination that is tantamount to a temptation to avoid understanding. The Lord of the Flies tries first to divert him from understanding by telling him he is 'just a silly little boy'; then the voice warns him to 'get back to the others', then cajoles him with promises to 'forget the whole thing', and finally seeks to frighten him off with the threat of 'doing' him - a threat that proves prophetic. But Simon refuses to forgo understanding by becoming one of the mob, tempting though this may be; he will not pretend that the killing is part of 'having fun', when he realises that it is an upshot of 'mankind's essential sickness'; he knows the Lord of the Flies is no more than a 'pig's head on a stick', its voice a ventriloquisation of what is going on in his own mind. The stress of this leads to his having a fit, but weak as he is when he regains consciousness, he climbs the mountain and crawls forward to *examine* (Golding's word) 'the white nasal bones, the teeth, the colours of corruption'. He vomits with revulsion, but he understands; and typically, his compassion is aroused, so that he releases the 'poor body' of the dead airman from 'the wind's indignity'.

Finally, Simon tries to bring his discovery that the Beast is 'harmless and horrible' to the others, but they are in a frenzy and destroy him. Ironically, his truth goes unheard to the very end. But if he is the victim of the 'essential sickness' in the other boys, his broken, huddled body is beautified by nature, and assimilated to the grandeur of nature's processes, to which he was so responsive when alive.

Roger

A 'slight, furtive' boy, always grave, gloomy and humourless, Roger is a born sadist. In the early part of the novel, he mutters his name and is dark, taciturn and menacing. His psychology is never examined or explained.

In Chapter 4 we see him leading the way straight through the sandcastles, 'kicking them over, burying the flowers, scattering the chosen stones'. His satisfaction lies in spoiling the littluns' game. He lingers to watch Henry become absorbed 'beyond mere happiness' as he plays with the 'transparencies' that scavenge the beach. Some falling coconuts suggest to Roger not his own danger, but a menacing game of his own. He throws stones that only just miss Henry. As Golding says, Roger's arm 'was conditioned by a civilisation that knew nothing of him'; but this conditioning quickly weakens. The violence of rolling rocks fascinates Roger, and when Ralph is anxious to get a fire going, Roger defies him, wanting to topple the rocks of Castle Rock (Chapter 6).

When Ralph and Jack climb the mountain in Chapter 7, Roger silently joins them. This takes courage, even if when they creep forward towards the Beast, Roger lags a little (though less, finally, than Jack). We see Roger most actively himself when the sow is killed in Chapter 8. His spear is cruelly forced up the pig's anus, and there are overtones of his being sexually excited, as if by a perverted rape. Though 'uncommunicative by nature' he speaks the crude words that release the boys' tension: 'Right up her ass!' But it is Jack who brings about Roger's final 'illumination', by arbitrarily beating Wilfred. From this point on, Roger abandons all restraint, all memory of civilised standards. His sadism is released unchecked, and he becomes overtly a killer and torturer. He topples the rock that kills Piggy 'with a sense of delirious abandonment'; his enthusiasm for torturing Sam and Eric is so compulsive that he edges past Jack, 'only just avoiding pushing him with his shoulder', and it is Roger who sharpens the stick at both ends for Ralph. The twins know to their cost that he is 'a terror', and we are told that 'the hangman's horror clings around him'. He is cast in the same mould as the Nazi commandants of Belsen and Auschwitz and is fulfilled only when he wields an authority that is 'nameless' and 'irresponsible'.

Maurice

Maurice follows Roger in kicking over the littluns' sandcastles but has enough vestigial civilisation and decency to feel an impulse to apologise. He relives the tense antagonism between Ralph and Jack (Chapter 4) by acting the part of a pig, in a re-enactment of the killing, and does much the same by diverting the littluns with his clowning (Chapter 5). However, his talk of squids 'hundreds of yards long' does little to soothe the littluns' terrors, and he contributes to the making of tribal ritual by suggesting that the savages' dance should be done properly, with a drum accompaniment.

Sam and Eric

Since they are identical twins who feel, think and act alike, Golding emphasises their essential unity by making a compound 'Samneric' out of their separate names. Even their talk is antiphonal, one completing whatever the other says. They are by nature cheerful, easy-going and good-natured, though rather too easily influenced. While happy to help Ralph and keep the fire, they abandon their duty to join Jack's hunters, and are given the chore of carrying the carcass of the pig. Their panic at seeing what they imagine is a Beast is extreme, and their account of it very highly coloured. Because of their essential decency, they support Ralph, preferring him to Jack; but their polite, middle-class exclamations, 'out of the heart of civilisation', cannot save them from being captured by Jack, to whom they at least *attempt* to be loyal out of fear. They do not willingly betray Ralph, but do so under torture. There is nothing heroic about them: they are *average* boys, too shallow to face up to their part in Simon's death, too weak to withstand pain, too malleable to resist Jack. They represent ordinary humanity, the crowd and the masses.

Percival

One of the very smallest of the boys, Percival is unattractive, badly adjusted and whimpers from having sand kicked in his eyes by Roger and Maurice; but he is similarly persecuted by the other littluns, Henry and Johnny, too. Pushed into the assembly by the littluns, he pathetically recites his name, address and telephone number, though by the end of the story he has forgotten even his name. He is shown as weeping and wailing even in his sleep, and is tormented by nightmares in which he lives 'through circumstances in which the incantation of his address is powerless to help him'. Percival has a reputation for being 'batty' because of his odd behaviour and constant crying, but he is in fact a figure of pathos.

5.3 STYLE

There are two fundamental and related questions we must ask about the style of any novel. First, what is the author's attitude to his readers? Second, what is the author's attitude to his materials?

Lord of the Flies is remarkable for its author's detachment. Golding tells his story with vividness and economy, but keeps himself well out of it. There are no intrusions of the kind found in Dickens and many living novelists, who permit themselves to comment on the characters and plots they invent. On the contrary, Golding appears to write impersonally, unfolding his story without moralising and with apparent neutrality. There is no attempt on his part to alert the reader to the horrors he describes, and no indication that his own emotions are involved in what he so painstakingly records. But we should not be deceived by this. We know that Golding set out to expose Ballantyne's idealised *Coral Island* for a fake, and because his story is a 'fable' we can be certain that he foresaw its outcome from the start – an outcome that is profoundly moralising, even if the question of morality is never directly or explicitly raised. *Lord of the Flies* has all the appearance of being straightforward narrative, but this is simply a novelist's device, cleverly handled by Golding. His art is to conceal art.

Formally, Golding writes as the 'omniscient author', which means he chooses not to write the story from the point of view of one of its characters, but to write it with the detachment of someone who surveys all the characters, and all the action, all the time, from a vantage point the reader is permitted to share. But this too, is deceptive, since at certain points in the novel he obliges the reader to identify with his characters, and does this by cutting out all words except those directly relating to what the *characters themselves* use, or think, or feel. In the first chapter, for example, Ralph, Jack and Simon are toppling a rock:

'Heave!'
Sway back and forth, catch the rhythm.
'Heave!'
Increase the swing of the pendulum, increase, increase, come up and bear against that point of furthest balance – increase – increase –
'Heave!'

This, far from being an objective account, is an account perceived subjectively, from inside the skin of the boys themselves. Or consider how we are made to share the terrors of Ralph in the last chapter:

'Think.'
What was the sensible thing to do? . . .
Break the line.
A tree.
Hide, and let them pass. . .
Don't scream.
You'll get back.
Now he's seen you, he's making sure. A stick sharpened.

The language is reduced to essentials only. It is all that we are given, and we cannot but make it our own and so identify with Ralph, whose internal dialogue it is.

When we turn to Golding's attitude to his materials, we again find it to be formal, and *apparently* uninvolved and objective. There are no explicit comments on the action, however horrifying it may be; there is no overt approval of the good, or criticism of the bad, characters. Indeed, the aloofness of the author from both action and characters is often reinforced by his use of images that seem to distance and reduce what happens to virtual insignificance. When, for example, the boys discover Castle Rock, Golding notes that the neck of land connecting it to the island will be eroded by the sea 'soon, in a matter of centuries'. The perspective of time is on an even grander, evolutionary scale when, at the beginning of Chapter 3, Jack is shown naked on all fours and 'ape-like' in a shadowy forest disturbed by a bird that rises from its 'primitive nest' with 'a harsh cry that seemed to come out of the abyss of ages'. The tide that claims Simon's body is deliberately related to cosmic images:

> Somewhere over the darkened curve of the world the sun and
> moon were pulling; and the film of water on the earth planet
> was held, bulging slightly on one side while the solid core turned.

The vast scale of such images reinforces the elemental and universal
themes that Golding explores (man and man's nature and his place in
the scheme of things); but the author's detachment and objectivity are
more apparent than real. When they have killed Simon, it is said of the
boys: 'Even in the rain they could see how small a beast it was. . .'. This
smallness, set against the majesty of the cosmic forces, serves only to
deepen and enrich the pathos we feel. Or consider Piggy's death:

> Piggy fell forty feet and landed on his back across the square, red
> rock in the sea. His head opened and stuff came out and turned
> red. Piggy's arms and legs twitched a bit, like a pig's after it has
> been killed.

The directness and simplicity of this is obvious. No moral tone is evi-
dent. The second sentence is heavily monosyllabic and adopts a kind of
schoolboy idiom, with 'stuff' used at the crucial point. Even here, at a
tragic climax, Golding risks a bad pun and bad joke by the analogy he
draws between Piggy and the animal he is named after. Detachment
could hardly go further. So how can we account for the tragic impact
that the account of Piggy's death makes? Surely it comes precisely from
the assumed detachment, and even callousness, of the author, who
refuses to weaken his effects by coming between the action and the
reader, and allows the facts to speak starkly and horrifyingly for themselves.

The novel begins and ends abruptly, and develops at a rapid pace,
allowing for a few flash-backs that establish, in sharp contrast to the
savagery of the island, the secure middle-class world Ralph comes from.
In general, the sentences are short, though varied in structure, and
where they are long and more elaborate, as in the description of the
tide that claims Simon's body, they slow to a majestic pace for obvious
reasons. The abrupt, broken, exclamatory sentences of Ralph, when he
is hunted down, are no less functional and appropriate in their context.

The dialogue, rich with the rather dated schoolboy slang of the post-
war period, is natural and convincing. Golding's psychological understanding of his characters extends to their use of language. Simon's
hesitancy and incoherence relate to his shyness and to an intuition that
puts too great a strain on words; Jack's sentences are abruptly expressed,
conveying a man of action's impatience with language; Piggy is distin-
guished by his plebeian speech, but this is often sustained through
several sentences, in keeping with his intellectual pretentions, whereas

the other boys typically speak in single or fragmentary sentences, and this is particularly true of Sam and Eric, who think and speak so alike that one of them is constantly completing what the other begins to say. The slang they habitually use binds the boys together, and so too does the ritual chanting; but we should note that once Jack becomes Chief, he requires his savages to speak to him, and about him, in a language that is formal and impersonal.

5.4 IMAGERY

The power of the novel resides in the power of its language, and Golding's language is remarkable for its precision, vividness and impact. *Lord of the Flies* uses a wide range of formal figures of speech; but more importantly, it uses them functionally and with poetic intensity, so that they come to us laden with significance. In the first chapter, for instance, where the island seems Eden-like, we are given a hint of menace and horror in the reference to 'skull-like coconuts' and the square black caps of the choirboys who perch 'like black birds' on the tree trunks near Ralph. Or consider how Eric, in Chapter 6, watches 'the scurrying wood-lice that were so frantically unable to avoid the flames' – an image that glances back to the fire that claimed the littlun in Chapter 2, and that points forward to the conflagration of the whole island in Chapter 12. Indeed, the images Golding uses, striking in themselves, are often repeated and integrated with related sets of images. For example, the 'quivering tangle of reflections from the lagoon' (Chapter 1) is matched by the 'tangle of golden reflections' (Chapter 5). Both these belong to the imagery of light, associated with common sense, and of darkness, associated with fear and superstition; and at the same time they relate to the mirage imagery, which Golding constantly uses to signal confusion between what is real and what is unreal. The 'tangle of golden reflections' quickly sets Ralph asking himself what a face is, or indeed, what *anything* is.

Listing striking figures of speech in *Lord of the Flies* is an easy matter. There are numerous instances connected with the sow, for example (Chapter 8). It is a 'bloated bag of fat', with a 'great bladder' of a belly, 'fringed with a row of piglets'; its guts look 'like a heap of glistening coal' and are surrounded by flies that buzz 'like a saw'; its skull seems 'to jeer...cynically', and its 'grin', when Ralph strikes it, breaking it in two pieces, expands to be 'six feet across'. But however telling such figurative language may be, the images employed have a resonance and significance that point far beyond themselves, and are, in fact, contributory to the novel's central symbol of the Lord of the

Flies, on to which the boys' fear and loathing and savagery and hatred are all projected. Though brilliantly realised in their physical details, the images add up to something that wholly transcends the overt reality they depict. Golding's genius lies precisely in his ability to portray abstract moral and metaphysical themes in sensuous, and seemingly every-day, language. His art is to invest apparently natural objects and events with an enriching imagery, implying a new dimension of meaning, and it is this we refer to as symbolism.

6 SPECIMEN PASSAGE

AND COMMENTARY

Specimen passage from Chapter 9

Again the blue-white scar jagged above them and the sulphurous explosion beat down. The littluns screamed and blundered about, fleeing from the edge of the forest, and one of them broke the ring of biguns in his terror.

"Him! Him!"

The circle became a horseshoe. A thing was crawling out of the forest. It came darkly, uncertainly. The shrill screaming that rose before the beast was like a pain. The beast stumbled into the horseshoe.

"Kill the beast! Cut his throat! Spill his blood!"

The blue-white scar was constant, the noise unendurable. Simon was crying out something about a dead man on a hill.

"Kill the beast! Cut his throat! Spill his blood! Do him in!"

The sticks fell and the mouth of the new circle crunched and screamed. The beast was on its knees in the centre, its arms folded over its face. It was crying out against the abominable noise something about a body on the hill. The beast struggled forward, broke the ring and fell over the steep edge of the rock to the sand by the water. At once the crowd surged after it, poured down the rock, leapt on to the beast, screamed, struck, bit, tore. There were no words, and no movements but the tearing of teeth and claws.

Then the clouds opened and let down the rain like a waterfall. The water bounded from the mountain-top, tore leaves and branches from the trees, poured like a cold shower over the struggling heap on the sand. Presently the heap broke up and figures staggered away. Only the beast lay still, a few yards from the sea. Even in the rain they could see how small a beast it was; and already its blood was staining the sand.

Now a great wind blew the rain sideways, cascading the water from the forest trees. On the mountain-top the parachute filled and moved; the figure slid, rose to its feet, spun, swayed down through a vastness of wet air and trod with ungainly feet the tops of the high trees; falling, still falling, it sank towards the beach and the boys rushed screaming into the darkness. The parachute took the figure forward, furrowing the lagoon, and bumped it over the reef and out to sea.

Towards midnight the rain ceased and the clouds drifted away, so that the sky was scattered once more with the incredible lamps of stars. Then the breeze died too and there was no noise save the drip and trickle of water that ran out of clefts and spilled down, leaf by leaf, to the brown earth of the island. The air was cool, moist, and clear; and presently even the sound of the water was still. The beast lay huddled on the pale beach and the stains spread, inch by inch.

The edge of the lagoon became a streak of phosphorescence which advanced minutely, as the great wave of the tide flowed. The clear water mirrored the clear sky and the angular bright constellations. The line of phosphorescence bulged about the sand grains and little pebbles; it held them each in a dimple of tension, then suddenly accepted them with an inaudible syllable and moved on.

Along the shoreward edge of the shallows the advancing clearness was full of strange, moonbeam-bodied creatures with fiery eyes. Here and there a larger pebble clung to its own air and was covered with a coat of pearls. The tide swelled in over the rain-pitted sand and smoothed everything with a layer of silver. Now it touched the first of the stains that seeped from the broken body and the creatures made a moving patch of light as they gathered at the edge. The water rose further and dressed Simon's coarse hair with brightness. The line of his cheek silvered and the turn of his shoulder became sculptured marble. The strange, attendant creatures, with their fiery eyes and trailing vapours, busied themselves round his head. The body lifted a fraction of an inch from the sand and a bubble of air escaped from the mouth with a wet plop. Then it turned gently in the water.

Somewhere over the darkened curve of the world the sun and moon were pulling; and the film of water on the earth planet was held, bulging slightly on one side while the solid core turned. The great wave of the tide moved further along the island and the water lifted. Softly, surrounded by a fringe of inquisitive bright creatures, itself a silver shape beneath the steadfast constellations, Simon's dead body moved out towards the open sea.

Commentary

The passage is taken from the heart of the novel. It is no exaggeration to say that if Simon's death is not properly understood, the novel as a whole cannot be properly understood.

Chapter 9 begins with a powerful, almost meteorological description of heat and humidity that build up, stiflingly and ominously, to their explosive release in a tropical storm. Parallel with this, there is a rising tension in the action, which reaches its own climax and release in the savage murder of Simon. The 'blue-white scar' of the lightning 'jags' (a simple but telling coinage of Golding's) above the heads of the boys, who have formed a ring and have lost their identities in dancing frenziedly to the rhythms of a mindless chant. They have become part of 'the throb and stamp of a single organism', absorbed in mob terror and violence, and are no longer individuals. The 'sulphurous explosion' that beats down on them has appropriate suggestions of Hell, as does the pained screaming of the littluns, so that by extension the boys appear as devils.

They dance on a strip of sand by the sea. Behind it is the dark forest, which they hold in superstitious dread, believing that a destructive Beast lurks there. The ring of bigger boys is broken, so becoming a horseshoe, and at this point a 'thing' crawls out of the forest into its 'mouth', which crunches and screams as it fastens on the 'thing'. It is worth noting that Golding uses the words 'thing' and 'beast', together with the possessive pronoun 'its' ('The beast was on its knees...its arms folded over its face') when describing Simon as he is perceived by his murderers. This emphasises the anonymity of the 'thing'. In their frenzy, the boys, who are themselves without identity, cannot identify Simon or even recognise him as a boy. They have projected onto him their own obliterating terror. When, therefore, Golding uses Simon's name, the author's objective perception is set alongside the subjective perception of the boys, so that the event is presented to the reader in what amounts to a twofold perspective.

Simon cries out 'something about a body on the hill', but his voice cannot be heard. Here, again and for the last time, he struggles to communicate to the other boys a knowledge of vital importance to them. But just as, in the assemblies, he was never given hearing when he stammered out the truth that the Beast they fear is part of themselves, so now, when he brings them the truth of his discovery that the Beast inhabiting the mountain top is only a dead airman, his voice and the sanity it represents is drowned by the mindlessness of the chant. Simon's spiritual heroism in climbing the mountain, despite his physical exhaustion, resulted from his passionate and compassionate need to unveil and comprehend the truth. He vomits at the horror he discovers; but he realises it is a *human* horror, and in compassion he disentangles the strings that twitch the corpse like a puppet as the wind plays in the parachute, repeatedly jerking it into a mockery of resurrection. And no sooner does he do this, than out of concern for the others, he makes his way down the mountain, to share his discovery with them, and so declare the truth that will make them free of the Beast that in reality is only a projection of their own bestial fear and mass madness.

It is profoundly ironic that Simon, who is essentially a visionary and 'saint', should be mistaken for the Beast by the Beast itself, which is the mob violence of his destroyers. His message about 'a dead man on a hill', carries an obscure ambiguity (it refers to the dead airman, though it has overtones of Christ's crucifixion), but this is drowned by both the thunder and the boys' screaming. The mouth of the circle of boys is, in fact, the mouth of the true Beast, though the word 'beast' is repeatedly used in reference to Simon alone: 'the beast was on its knees. . .' 'the beast struggled forward. . .'. Simon succeeds in wrenching himself free from the jaws of the real Beast, which, though it is never *called* a Beast, is described in terms that strongly imply animality: it 'surges' and 'pours' after Simon, 'leaps' on him, 'strikes, bites and tears'; and throughout there are 'no words' and 'no movements but the tearing of teeth and claws'. The power of the description comes from combining the monosyllabic strength of the vocabulary with the implicit image of the crowd as ravening animal.

The savagery of the crowd is released in murder. At the same time, the rain is released 'like a waterfall' and pours 'like a cold shower' on to the 'struggling heap' of boys, cooling their lust to kill and restoring them to consciousness. Significantly, once they regain consciousness, the 'heap' of boys breaks up, and it is individual 'figures' who are said to 'stagger away'. They stagger from physical exhaustion, but equally now under the burden of realising what it is that they have done. The sentences are short and the spare simplicity of the style evokes pathos: 'Even in the rain they could see how small a beast it was. . .'.

Golding at this point gives us a respite from Simon's destruction, and turns detachedly to another release that parallels the release of the rain and the release of the boys' murderous violence. A short, new paragraph changes subject with the abrupt simplicity often found in biblical prose: 'Now a great wind blew the rain sideways. . .'. And lifted by this 'great wind', the parachute fills and bears the dead airman, a sad symbol of war and man's inhumanity to man, across the island and lagoon, to its burial in the open sea. There are two striking features in the writing.

One is the intensely realised detail: the airman's feet 'tread' 'the tops of
the high trees', and 'furrow' the lagoon. The other feature is the remarkable enactment of the action in the rhythms of the prose itself:

> ...the figure slid, rose to its feet, spun, swayed down through a
> vastness of wet air...falling, still falling, it sank towards the
> beach...

Although no mention is made of Simon, this release of the dead airman
is none the less Simon's posthumous last act – typically an act of
humanity and compassion.

The next paragraph marks the passing of time. Rain and clouds
depart, the breeze dies, the 'drip and trickle of water' (an onomatopoeic
relic from the storm) ceases, and Simon's body, still ironically referred
to as 'the beast's body', lies in a spreading stain of blood under 'the
incredible lamps of stars'. It is 'huddled', a word suggesting its defensive
curling up against its attackers, while recapturing the previously evoked
pathos, and its smallness is set against the huge magnificence of the
stars, so initiating the sustained imagery of contrasting scales of vision.
Although it is 'towards midnight', there is repeated emphasis on the
clarity that has supplanted the stifling darkness of the storm: the air
has become 'cool, moist and clear', and 'the clear water' mirrors 'the
clear sky', while the tide is an 'advancing clearness'. But this clarity is
not simply physical. It is like a restoration of sanity after madness, and
illuminates an understanding of all that has happened in the novel. It
is, moreover, associated with beauty, while beauty itself is associated
with Simon's dead body.

Exploiting the strength of simple monosyllables still, Golding describes the flow of 'the great wave of the tide', which gently claims
Simon's body and draws it to the open sea. The tide is itself phosphor-
escent, 'full of strange, moonbeam-bodied creatures with fiery eyes' –
creatures that are as minute in comparison to Simon's body as Simon's
body is to the starry skies above him. And again we are given minutely
observed details that are normally realised with such intensity only in
poetry. The phosphorescence 'bulges' about sand grains, and holds
pebbles in 'a dimple of tension', so that they cling to their own air and
are covered with 'a coat of pearls'. It touches the bloodstains, Simon's
'broken body' (an expression with overtones of martyrdom and even
crucifixion), and 'dresses' his coarse hair with a 'brightness' that corresponds to a saint's halo. The use of the verb 'dress' suggests a deliberate
act, and this is reinforced by the way the 'strange, attendant creatures',
like servants attentive to their master's corpse, busy themselves in
silvering the line of Simon's cheek and shoulder, transforming him into
an effigy of 'sculptured marble'. It is as if nature in all its variety, from

tiny organisms to the tidal swell of the vast ocean, pays homage to a martyr by glorifying his remains.

In the last paragraph, the scale of vision shifts from the microscopic creatures paying a last tribute to Simon to a cosmic perspective, whereby the ocean itself is seen as no more than a 'film of water' on the 'darkened curve' of the planet Earth. But while Golding certainly shows us how insignificant mankind and his world are, on a cosmic scale, he concludes with the image of Simon's body moving out to the ocean, surrounded by 'a fringe of inquisitive bright creatures'. Simon, who passionately loved nature, is carried out to sea (itself a symbol of eternity), and is assimilated to the majestic processes of the universe, which holds in a web of interconnection both grains of sand and the 'steadfast constellations', the 'moonbeam-bodied creatures' and the gravitational pull of the sun and moon, the 'wet plop' of the bubble of air that escapes from Simon's mouth (a homely detail that does not detract from the sustained beauty of the description) and the remote silence of the 'incredible lamps of stars'. No finer tribute could be paid to Golding's art than to say that this passage invites comparison with William Wordsworth's 'A Slumber Did My Spirit Steal', a great, simple poem in which the poet represents the dead child, Lucy, as being gathered back into the majestic but impersonal processes of nature:

> No motion has she now, no force;
> She neither hears nor sees;
> Rolled round in earth's diurnal course,
> With rocks, and stones, and trees.

7 CRITICAL RECEPTION

Lord of the Flies is the most popular and best-selling of William Golding's many novels, and has met with world-wide acclaim, but its success was by no means immediate. Before Faber and Faber accepted it, the novel had been rejected by twenty or more publishers, and although it appeared in 1954, its sales were initially modest. When it did finally achieve success, it did so on a spectacular scale, becoming a 'cult' book during the 1960s, with an immense readership in schools, colleges and universities throughout the English-speaking world. Penguin Books gave it a place in their list of Modern Classics, numerous Examining Boards prescribed it for study, and Peter Brook turned it into an award-winning film in 1963.

Although several of the early reviews of *Lord of the Flies* accorded generous recognition to Golding's talent, the book received a mixed reception. To this day, widely differing views are held as to its merits, some critics objecting that the book is too facile and fashionable in its pessimism. The fact is that *Lord of the Flies* is unmistakably about human nature and the human condition; it is a kind of fable, but it is a fable so completely realised that it permits a wide range of possible interpretations, corresponding more or less to the different convictions and expectations of its readers.

Some critics have been severe on *Lord of the Flies* because it seems to them that the book does not, like most good novels, grow convincingly out of the characters and situation. They charge Golding with being too intent on proving a thesis by shaping his materials towards a preconceived outcome, and the implication is that the story fails to have the organic structure of a novel, and substitutes for it the mechanical structure of a fable. In this reading, Simon is criticised for being unrealistic and a mere device for enabling the author to state his own point of view. Other critics strongly deny this, arguing that the story and fable are not simply compatible, but so perfectly integrated as to be inseparable. Situation and characters and narrative are held to be entirely convincing at a naturalistic level, while simultaneously embodying the deeper truths of the fable.

But critics have disagreed in their views of what the novel's deeper truths are. It is easy enough to read into the struggle between Ralph and Jack a political clash between democracy and Fascism. However, liberal critics have denounced the novel for what they consider to be its commitment to the Christian doctrine of 'original sin'. This is a charge that is difficult to sustain, even if it is fair to allow that the novel is profoundly pessimistic. The pig's spiked head has been taken by some readers for Beelzebub, the Devil, but this again is disputable, and most critics are surely correct in suggesting that it, like the Beast itself, is no more than an object onto which the boys project the fear and hatred and evil that are not supernatural, but rather a part of themselves and of human nature generally.

Just as critics with a religious inclination saw *Lord of the Flies* as a religious fable concerned with the fallen condition of man and the loss of Eden, so critics who were psychologically inclined interpreted the novel in Freudian terms. Instead of a theological struggle between good and bad, Freudians analysed the struggle as taking place between the dark and violent forces of the unconscious (the Id), the rational principle (the Ego), and the moral conscience (the Super-Ego). Jack, Piggy and Ralph, and Simon were seen as representatives of these three aspects of the mind, and it was argued that the tragic events of the story resulted from the incomplete and unbalanced nature of the boys' characters, since none of them is sufficiently mature to achieve harmonious control of the mind's three constituents. Meanwhile, critics with sociological interests were less concerned about the divisive personalities of the boys, than about the disintegration of the group. Civilisation, they pointed out, provides whatever humane standards the group has, and as the group regresses, these standards are disastrously abandoned. This view upholds the necessity for authority, whether of parents, or the State, or the Church. But to critics with a taste for anthropology, what was most fascinating about the novel was the portrayal of the boys' regression. This was seen as reversing and abbreviating mankind's evolution, so affording insights into primitive society and the way in which the savage mind creates taboos and rituals, demonologies and myths.

It ought to be said that all these critical approaches to the novel have at least *some* validity, and this, properly appreciated, is a high tribute to its merits. All great art is characterised by its rich suggestiveness, by its potential to be variously interpreted, and by its capacity to challenge and upset readers who deceive themselves by supposing that artistic statement can be reduced to merely theoretical or ideological statement.

Lord of the Flies cannot be summed up in any single critical approach, or in a combination of many different critical approaches. Guided by intelligent criticism, we ought to be able to reach a better understanding of the novel, but its profound insights depend on the skill and power of Golding's writing, which is finally untranslatable into any other terms than its own.

REVISION QUESTIONS

1. Discuss the view that the novel is a sad commentary on human nature.

2. The action of the story should be seen in relation to a world destroyed by atomic war. Consider this view.

3. Education and the social order impose severe restrictions on people, but we cannot be human without them. Discuss, keeping in mind the degeneration of Golding's characters into savagery.

4. What is the importance of Simon in the story?

5. The novel's development is brought about by ever deepening revelations. Discuss.

6. 'Even in [Golding's] first novel, it is not explanation and conclusion, but imaginative impact which is finally memorable.' Do you agree?

7. Golding's genius lies in his ability to handle abstract moral and metaphysical themes in the sensuous images of everyday language. Comment on this.

8. Examine the relationship between Ralph and Jack.

9. Golding's boys are real boys, but they are more than that. Discuss.

10. 'The Child's world on the island is a painful microcosm of the adult world.' Discuss.